Move, Sing, Listen, Play
Preparing the young child for music

By DONNA WOOD

Acknowledgements

All around the buttercup by Denise Bacon
I see the moon by Denise Bacon
Fuzzy Wuzzy by Denise Bacon
©Copyright 1971 by Boosey & Hawkes Inc. Used by permission of Boosey (Canada) Ltd.

The big ship sails by Richard Chase
Used with the permission of Dover Publications, Inc., N.Y., and was taken from the book *Singing games and party games* by Richard Chase 1967.

Hallowe'en is pumpkin time by Lucile Panabaker
Everything's sleeping by Lucile Panabaker
The orchestra is playing by Lucile Panabaker
Used by permission of Stoddart Publishing Co. Limited, Don Mills, Ontario.

Here sits the monkey From AMERICAN FOLK SONGS FOR CHILDREN,
by Ruth Crawford Seeger, Doubleday/Zephyr. Used by permission.

Pony song by Satis N. Coleman and Alice G. Thorn
Lyrics and melody of "Pony Song" from *Singing time: Songs for nursery and school* by Satis N. Coleman and Alice G. Thorn.
Copyright 1929 by Satis N. Coleman and Alice G. Thorn. Renewed 1957 by Satis N. Coleman and Horace E. Thorn.
A John Day book. By permission of Thomas Y. Crowell, publishers.

Roll my ball
English translation of *En roulant ma boule* from *Music is motion* by Edna G. Buttolph. By permission of The Willis Music Co., Florence, KY.

A special thank you to Oriole Nursery School, Toronto, and the Royal Conservatory of Music for offering me the challenge.

I thank the parents and the children who appear in the photographs throughout the book.

Design: Ron Butler
Layout: Kerri Weller
Cover: First Image

Printed in Canada

To my husband, Bob

About the author

Donna Wood is a graduate of the Royal Conservatory of Music, Toronto. She is also a certified Early Childhood Educator, Institute of Child Study, University of Toronto. After many years of practical experience in inner-city, day care and co-op nursery schools, she introduced and developed *Preparatory Music Classes* at the Royal Conservatory of Music for children aged 3 to 7 and *Music with your Baby* for parents and their children aged 6-36 months. For many years, Donna Wood directed summer school courses and academic year courses in teacher training. In 1987, The Association for Early Childhood Education, Ontario (ECE) presented her with the Children's Service Award and medal for outstanding contributions toward improving the quality of life for young children. In 1991, she helped develop and promote an advanced cross-disciplinary Early Childhood Music Education Certificate, through Ryerson Polytechnical University's School of Early Childhood Education (Division of Continuing Education) and the Royal Conservatory of Music. As a leader in the field of Early Childhood Music Education, Donna Wood has conducted many workshops and seminars across Canada for teachers, caregivers and parents. She has also presented papers at the International Society of Music Education (ISME) in U.S.A., Austria, Hungary, Australia and Finland.

Contents

Preface

To turn young children towards music, to help them discover what music is through personal experience and then to encourage them to make their own music can be an exciting challenge for a teacher. But it is a difficult challenge and the teacher must gather, study, and adapt methods and materials that will be effective in this work. We look for the kind of musical learning that offers the greatest possibilities to the individual child. Out-going, physically active children may learn best with music and vigorous movement activities − they can have many musical experiences if the teacher is able to stimulate, direct and control this interest. Another child will find music in the sound and rhythms of speech. Some will discover the joy of singing, and others will be stimulated when making sounds with instruments. I believe that an effective music curriculum should offer all of these activities, so that all children may be turned towards music.

In this book, I will suggest methods and materials for teaching children, from birth to seven years of age. There are also many games to teach the elements of music, through movement, speech, singing, listening and the playing of instruments: Thus, the teacher will have a variety of activities from which to choose.

Is it better for the early childhood music educator to be a trained musician with an interest in teaching young children or is it better to be an early childhood teacher with an interest in teaching music? I believe that the enthusiastic teacher can gain insights and skills in both disciplines and thereby contribute to the musical enrichment of the young child.

No matter what method is used, it is the teacher who "makes the difference." In the last section of this book, I have tried to offer a variety of musical and pedagogical "know how," so that the teacher will gain confidence and skill − and so enjoy the process of making music with young children.

Donna Wood, 1982

Preface to Expanded Edition

I would like to thank many colleagues and students who have used *Move, Sing, Listen, Play* and made helpful comments about the contents. This new edition gives me a welcome opportunity to give a special thank-you to teacher, Mary Stouffer, Professor Donald McKay, typist, Joyce Kenno, and editor, Kathy Bidell, for their strong support in this expanded and revised edition.

Donna Wood
Consultant Faculty
The Royal Conservatory of Music
1995

PART I
The child

Child development – Music development

Modern music educators such as Dalcroze, Kodaly and Orff first developed their philosophies and methods for older children. Then, working *backwards*, they gradually realized that preparatory work with younger children was important.

On the other hand, the early childhood educator is concerned with the development of the child from birth. We *start at the beginning* and work *forwards*.

I believe that the music teacher must also think of the "beginning" in order to work effectively with the young child. Music teachers must have a knowledge of what young children are really like – their general characteristics, behaviour, growth and development, in order to foster a love of music in each child.

Though the perceptive teacher will always consider the "whole child," some developmental areas are of particular importance to the music teacher.

1. Active learning (through play)

2. Social development

3. Language development

4. Creativity and Imagination

The following basic tenets of each of these areas must be considered by the teacher when selecting and preparing environment, equipment, musical material, methods and procedures.

Learning

All children can learn. Learning depends partly on mental capacity, partly on environment and partly on physical growth and development. The child must want to learn and be willing to continue trying, despite inevitable failure and mistakes. Feelings of success stimulate future learning. Playing and learning go hand in hand – play is the child's "work". Activities in this book are called "games" rather than "exercises."

Social development

"One to one" musical play between parent and infant gives a warm and happy beginning. Later, music learning is very often a group activity led by a teacher. For the class to go well, the teacher must understand and promote social skills and be ready to help the shy, antisocial or inhibited child. Participating in a group, learning to share and take turns, being a leader at times, and a follower at others, are all social skills which promote musical learning in a group. These skills develop slowly as the child matures. The teacher must have empathy towards each child, but also have a sensitivity and understanding of group dynamics. To this must be added the ability to be fair *and* firm, combined with a quiet sense of humour.

Language development

Modern music education makes much use of language to teach the elements of music – beat, rhythms, timbre and phrasing.

Language development begins with the early babbling sounds of babyhood and the joyful responses to playful sounds and words from a close and caring adult. Early speech has a singing quality and the child speaks and sings, subconsciously, during play. The teacher or parent can stimulate speech and vocabulary development with "sound" and "word" plays, rhymes and chants. These stimulate vocal skills, especially singing, and their rhythms prepare the child's ear for the rhythms of music.

Imagination and creativity

"The primary purpose of music education, as Orff sees it, is the development of a child's creative faculty which manifests itself in the ability to improvise.

Arnold Walter in the Introduction to Music for Children, Book I – Doreen Hall

Early childhood teachers consider the creative activities of art or music to be as important as any other subject on the curriculum. All children are encouraged to participate in activities where their own ideas, thoughts and feelings can be expressed.

I think of two aspects of the creativity of the young child. First, there is improvising within a framework. It should be part of every lesson, in movement, singing and instrument activities.

"How can you move in your space?"

"Tell me about this picture with your singing voice."

"Choose an instrument to play with this poem – this song."

The child chooses, explores and experiments. These are valuable for musical and personal development.

Then there is the other aspect, when the child expresses a spontaneous, original thought or idea. Perhaps the child or the class can develop the idea. It may need some redirection, but we must be careful not to tamper with heavy hands, any more than we would with a child's painting. It is the process of creativity, not the product, that is important for the child. In this context, all children may be creators.

The first five stages

GENERAL CHARACTERISTICS
DEVELOPING MUSICAL INTEREST
SOME MUSICAL SAMPLES

"It is clear that children who experience a musically stimulating environment in early life have greater capacity for learning and enjoying music than other children. The general level of interest and achievement in music among young children could be raised by educating parents and teachers of preschoolers to cultivate musical sensitivity ... through natural musical expression such as singing, playing and moving to music."

Early childhood Musical Development Gene M. Simons MENC.

To prepare young children for music, parents and teachers should be aware of some general characteristics of children's growth and learning. They should know how to stimulate musical interest with a variety of musical activities and materials. I have arranged the following section into a learning sequence of five stages, but this does not mean that songs and games cannot be repeated and enjoyed over several years. Children are happy to sing and play well known games over and over again. This is an excellent way to build self-confidence and musical skills.

The early years are a period of tremendous growth and change, so it may be helpful to have a general guide of the "ages and stages" of learning, when planning a music curriculum. But we must remember that each child is an individual and will not fit exactly into one "stage." This general guide also indicates to the class teacher that there should not be too great an age span in the group and that the teacher-child ratio should be small.

The musical samples are selected from traditional finger plays, rhymes and nursery songs that have been played and sung by parents and grandparents in family music making for generations, thereby passing on a valuable and basic musical heritage. The child who is nourished by such music can easily be led into the world of greater music in the next stages. So, do not rush through or omit these first stages. Some modern well-meaning parents tell me that they are introducing their babies to music by playing recordings of symphonies and concertos to them. Hearing sound is a new experience to a new born child and it takes many years to develop listening skills necessary to enjoy a Beethoven symphony. Try to imagine how your favorite symphony would sound, if you could hear the dynamics, the rhythm and some of the melodies but *not any harmony* or chord progressions.

"Children of preschool age cannot yet experience any sort of harmony at all."

H. Moog: The Musical Experience of the Preschool Child

An appropriate element of music is suggested beside each musical activity. With very little effort, a parent or teacher could lead the child to experience these basic elements of music with this simple material. The melodies are written within the natural range of young children's voices, starting with a descending interval, to encourage them to sing. Sing the songs slowly, at the child's pace. There are also some listening songs with a larger range, to be sung by the adult, with the children joining in if they wish. Small repeated actions on the beat, help children sing better. These activities, that parents and young children can enjoy together, lay a good foundation for the future enjoyment of music and indeed, contribute to the development of the whole child.

Infants and toddlers (Birth to two years)

GENERAL CHARACTERISTICS

Learning

Learning begins at birth. The child learns new skills by practising and repeating them many times. Routines of bathing and feeding, with a warm and loving adult, promote learning. A small but changing variety of toys stimulate intellectual development, physical development and hand-eye co-ordination. Floor play encourages them to explore their world with their bodies, preparing for whole body "movement and music" experiences.

Social development

From birth, the baby recognizes and shows interest in the human face, especially the mother's face. By three months old, there is social interaction between the baby and people around him. Babies react best to indivdual attention – patting, cuddling and rocking. Parents and others close to the infant, who show their joy in music, strongly influence the infant to also enjoy music.

Language

The baby listens with joy to playful sound and speech games initiated by the caring adult. This has a marked effect on speech development, and soon babies will respond with their own "sounds" and "words."

Imagination

The real world and immediate events take all their attention. By about twelve months, simple pictures and books will begin to show children the difference between the real and the imaginary world. They are not ready for fantasy.

DEVELOPING MUSICAL INTEREST

Moving

The infant's early experiences with movement and music through lullabies, dandling rhymes and traditional finger and foot "plays" make a happy beginning. The parent or infant-care worker who initiates some musical games every day, on a "one to one" basis, not only prepares the way for music education, but also adds to the quality of the child's life. Crawling, seat-sliding, rolling and toddling of the one year old, involve the whole body, preparing the child for active participation in "movement and music" games.

Singing

The pre-verbal stage is a crucial period for voice and language development. Babies who hear "live" speech and singing, respond with musical babbling, which later develops into speech and singing. Singing is a basic skill in modern music education. Talking and dandling games, singing and rocking lullabies are the beginning of music education. The adult should repeat simple nursery songs or sing spontaneous improvisations during caretaking routines.

Playing instruments

Choose rattles and bells that are safe and comfortable for the child to play. Too many different sounds are confusing. Sudden loud sounds may frighten the baby.

Listening

The father or mother who rocks and sings traditional folk songs and lullabies to the child is turning that child towards music. See p. 51, 52

"Why should anyone sing who has not been hushed to sleep by his mother's lullabies."

Kodaly

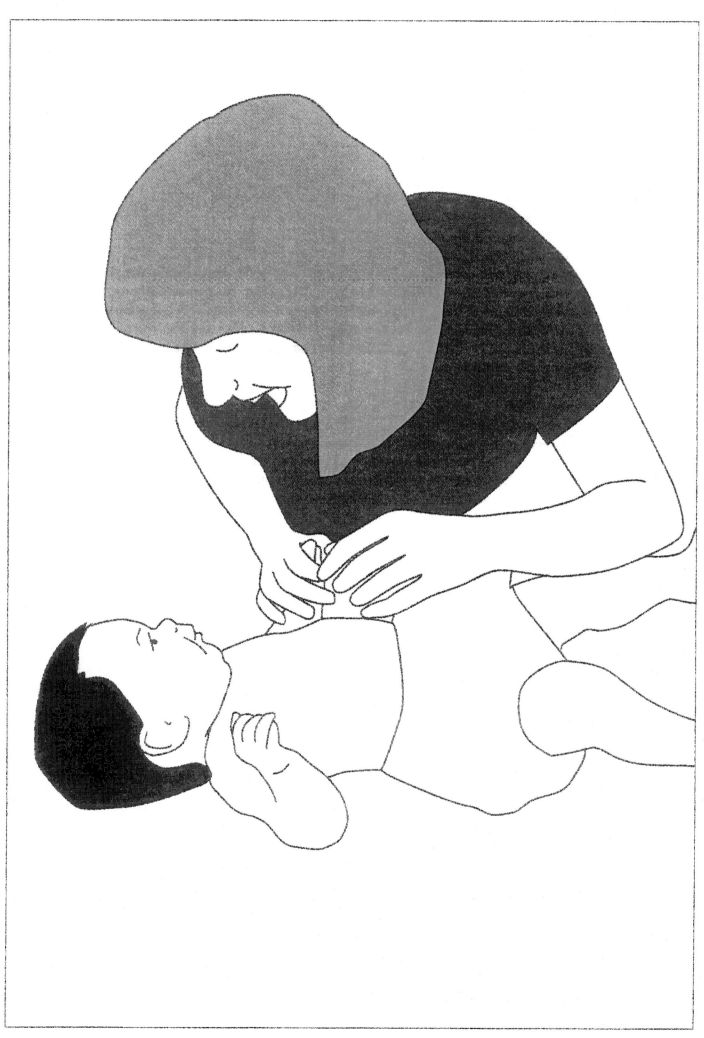

SOME MUSICAL SAMPLES

SPONTANEOUS IMPROVISATION while bathing, changing or dressing the baby

Listen

Hel-lo Bil-ly   peek-a-boo. where's your shoe? Here's your nose. Here's my nose.
Hel-lo Ju-lie   peek-a-boo. where's your shoe? Here's your nose. Here's my nose.

SPEECH PLAY

Beat
Shoe the old horse ᵀᵃᵖ   Tap baby's right foot *on the beat*

Shoe the old mare ᵀᵃᵖ   Tap baby's left foot *on the beat*

Let   little coltie go   Tap alternate feet, *on the beat*

Bare! Bare! Bare! ᵀᵃᵖ   Tap alternate feet, *on the beat*

The ᵀᵃᵖ allows a breathing space for the rest (𝄽)

SOUND PLAY

Timbre
What does the doggie say? Bow-wow-wow
How does the car go? Brrr-Brrr-Brrr
What does the wind say? Oooooooh

— continue with more questions and "sound" answers.

NURSERY SONG-GAME pat baby's hands on the beat

Beat

pat a cake ba - ker's man bake a cake as fast you can.

LULLABY: Always sing directly to the child with good "eye contact" as you rock on the beat

Slow beat

Bye oh— Ba - by ba - by Bye my lit - tle ba - by ba - by bye.

9

Two to three years

GENERAL CHARACTERISTICS

Learning
Two year olds like to find out about everything by touching, tasting, smelling, feeling and listening – not surprisingly, this is called "learning through the senses." Familiar, comfortable surroundings enhance the learning process at this age. They enjoy activities that can be repeated many times. They like a variety of toys but are confused by too many at the same time.

Social development
Two year olds are interested in other children, but are not ready to play "with" them. "Parallel play," beside others suits them better, where they are not required to share toys. With the sympathetic help of an adult, they might be able to participate in small group activity, but they should be free to join or to watch the activity.

Language
They understand simple directions and short explanations or pieces of information. They speak in single words or short sentences. The vocabulary is small, but they understand more words than they can say.

Imagination
Their thinking is concerned with the real world around them; though they might "pretend" to be something very familiar like a dog or a baby brother or sister.

DEVELOPING MUSICAL INTEREST

Moving
Two year olds enjoy moving their bodies to sounds and music with a firm regular beat. They bend knees, and swing arms with vigour. A running-walk oftens ends with a fall to the floor. The adult or teacher can encourage spontaneous movement with an accompaniment of mouth sounds (choo choo chug chug etc.) clapping or singing, picking up the child's "beat" if possible. Then the child may begin to get the feeling of "keeping the beat" with some one else.

Singing
Repeat finger plays, short rhymes, chants, games and songs with simple rhythmic texts, encouraging the child to "join in." The words and melody from your voice, unaccompanied, is better than a thumping piano accompaniment if you wish to develop musical singing in the child. They could learn to recognize and sing parts of about ten songs with an approximation of the melody, at this age.

Instruments
Instruments that the young child can hold and play easily can be introduced informally for short periods. Give maracas (rattles), small musical bells or jingles to the children to explore and experiment with, in their own way, and in their own time.

Listening
Encourage the child to listen, to name and to imitate sounds in the environment. Sing traditional nursery songs, folk songs, and composed songs of good quality to the child.

SOME MUSICAL SAMPLES

In these games the child is on the adult lap, face to face, or on a low chair or the floor, also face to face. It is important to keep a good eye contact with the child.

FINGER PLAY

Slowly-Quickly

Slowly, slowly very slowly creeps the garden snail,
Slowly, slowly very slowly up the garden rail.
Quickly quickly very quickly runs the little mouse.
Quickly quickly very quickly round about the house.

Game: adult "walks" fingers slowly, then quickly along child's arm and body.

SINGING GAME

Beat

Game: Hold child's hands up in front of face and peek around right, then left side, moving on the beat.

IMPROVISATIONS

Melody

Actions follow the words — improvise other short phrases to catch the "beat" of the activity.

SONG — Wee Willie Winkie

Listening

Three to four years

GENERAL CHARACTERISTICS

Learning
Children of three are ready for more structure and organization in their play. They like to look at and learn from picture and story books. There is a marked increase in attention span. Simple verbal directions and explanations can be understood.

Social development
Though still dependant on the adult, children of three are more interested in playing with other children and are more able to share and "take turns." But do not expect too much. A music group with about ten children is possible. Fifteen minute music periods every day are better than a long period once a week. As with two year olds, lead gently into music activities, without forcing.

Language
Clearer speech, a growing vocabulary and longer sentences are evident. Occasionally speech problems occur at this stage which must be handled with tact. Do not imitate or "make fun" of mistakes in pronunciation. The adult can foster speech maturation by using quiet, clear and interesting speech and generally being a good "model." High, childish speech mannerisms used by some adults when speaking to children, are *not* appropriate. The three year old loves to talk and also enjoys repeating words in a rhythmical way.

Imagination
Children of three to four are ready for and enjoy some fantasy and imaginative play, but cannot always differentiate between what is real and what is fantasy.

DEVELOPING MUSICAL INTEREST

Moving

The three year old enjoys walking, galloping, jumping and moving on the floor. Despite differences in physical development within the group, try to find a common tempo (not a regular feeling for beat, yet) when accompanying these activities with spontaneous singing, a drum or the piano. Develop ideas and suggestions of the children.

Singing

Encourage spontaneous speech patterns and singing throughout the day and also in short "organized" music sessions. Pitch, pronunciation and word sequence are uncertain because these skills develop slowly. Be tactful with children who have not "found" their singing voices. Repeat familiar songs and gradually introduce new ones. A simple repeated rhythmical action such as clapping, patting, pointing or swinging encourages and supports the singing. *Too many* complicated actions, often invented and used by the adult, will inhibit the singing of the child.

Instruments

Introduce instruments that produce sound vibrations from metal, wood or skin (bells, rhythm sticks, drums) to help the child to recognize and listen for contrasting tone quality (timbre). Name the instruments and talk a little about differences. Offer *each* child in the group an instrument — ten, inexpensive but musical jingles are better than one expensive instrument. Encourage spontaneity, experimenting and short "free play" experiences. Noisy banging is *not* music. Keeping the "beat" is not important yet — do not expect a co-ordinated group sound.

Listening

Encourage the children to listen and to pay attention, during short music sessions and ask them to listen, imitate and differentiate between contrasting voice sounds (animals, birds, machines, etc.). Sing songs of good musical quality about animals or people, to the child. If we wish to develop a sensitive musical taste in children, then we must use only good musical material.

CAN YOU WALK? CAN YOU STOP?

Sound The teacher claps, sings, or plays a hand drum, following the natural tempo of the children. "Let's see what we can see!"

Silence "When I *stop* the sound (clap or drum), you *stop* walking"

Repeat with galloping, and jumping in one place.

HOW CAN YOU MOVE ON THE FLOOR?

Tempo Can you be an engine? The children move on hands and knees chanting "choo! choo! choo! choo! Change tempo for a slower or a faster engine (Drum accompaniment). Can you tell when the train is going to stop? (Drum gets gradually slower)

COUNTING GAME – FINGER PLAY

Divided beat One potato, Two potato, Three potato, Four!

Five potato, Six potato, Seven potato, More!

"Make your hands into fists – these are the potatoes. Pile one potato on top of the other, as you count them, on the beat. The pile gets higher and then – they all fall down. Now, lets count and pile them up again.

NURSERY SONG

Slow beat
2/4 meter

Bob - by Shaf-to's gone to sea, sil - ver buc-kles on his knee,
He'll come back and mar -ry me, bon - ny Bob - by Shaf - to.

Rock the boat gently; on the beat
Follow with "Sea Shell" for mixed meter $\frac{2}{4} - \frac{6}{8}$. Repeat "Bobby" for A.B.A. Form

RESTING SONG

Slow beat
6/8 meter

Sea shell, Sea shell, sing a song to me.____

Sing a - bout the o - cean, Tell me a - bout the sea.____

Four to five years

GENERAL CHARACTERISTICS

Learning

Four year olds are eager to learn about their environment and the people in it. They ask many questions about what they see around them, but they are also curious and full of questions about the world beyond. Their attention span is longer and they play with more direction. If they have had some happy musical experiences, they are more ready to learn some basic concepts of music, if presented at their level.

Social development

Because the four year old is growing and learning at a rapid rate, there are often problems. Sometimes they are independent, reliable, co-operative and considerate – generally quite mature. At other times, they are helpless, unreliable, negative and selfish – decidedly immature. The appropriate music activity can have a therapeutic effect. Despite some stormy moments, they enjoy social activities and their friends.

Language

As well as asking questions, four year olds are eager to talk about what they know and think. With stimulation and encouragement, their vocabulary will grow at a rapid rate. They have a unique sense of humour, so nonsense rhymes or words with funny sounds have special appeal. The music teacher uses this interest to teach rhythm patterns and timbre.

Imagination

They have a lively imagination and know what "pretending" means. They like "to be" an animal or a machine and will say "I am a dog" – not "I am pretending to be a dog". The teacher must be aware of this seemingly fine point of difference. Let the child decide about "dressing up" – some are delighted to be a clown with a funny hat – others are not ready, especially in a group situation. One item, i.e. a sash or a shawl, to suggest a character, seems better than an elaborate costume.

DEVELOPING MUSICAL INTEREST

Moving

Marching, stamping, hopping, sliding and twirling can be added to the movement repertoire. Body awareness and body control are developing. However, skipping, which requires hopping on alternate feet, is difficult or impossible for many four year olds. Give the child time to master this activity. They enjoy moving like animals and making animal sounds for accompaniment. Start with animals that children have seen for themselves, if you can. Large clear pictures are a substitute, but can you imagine "being" an elephant or a giraffe, if you have never seen a real one? Some nursery rhymes and folk songs are good for simple movement dramas e.g. "The three little kittens have lost their mittens"; but they should be short with the child or children deciding how to proceed. Repeat, so that all who wish to, can have an opportunity to "act".

Singing

Prepare the voice and develop a sense of rhythm, with finger plays, body plays, word chants and rhymes. As speech develops, introduce longer speech patterns, rhymes and songs to capture interest and stimulate musical learning. Include some material to appeal to the four year old's sense of humour and nonsense. Small repeated rhythmic actions make good accompaniments to singing.

Instruments

The musical concepts of loud/soft and quick/slow can be introduced while exploring a greater variety of instruments. Tone bars (pitched) can be introduced for ear training and pitch games. Introduce children to the joy of ensemble playing as they walk, sing and play with jingle bells, maracas and hand drums. Well known songs such as "Jingle Bells" or "Baa Baa Black Sheep" work well, and a piano or drum accompaniment will hold it all together.

Listening

Sing "story" folk songs, encouraging children to "listen". Recordings of a solo voice or instrument are appropriate, if short. Young children are happy with the melody alone and do not hear the element of harmony, yet.

SOME MUSICAL SAMPLES

Move with the music

MOVING – Walk Walk Walk around   *Tennessee*

1. Walk, walk, walk a - round, walk a - round to - geth - er.
2. March, march, march a - round, . . .
3. Jump, jump, jump a - round, . . .
4. Gall - op, . . . (change meter)
5. Skip, skip, . . .
6. Slide, . . . (change meter)
7. Dance, dance, (¾ or ²⁄₄ meter.)

Walk, walk, walk a - round, walk a - round to - geth - er.

Finger play chant

SINGING – Jack and Jill

1. Jack and Jill went up the hill to fetch a pail of wa - ter,
2. Jack fell down and broke his crown and Jill came tumb-ling af - ter.

The children sit on the floor and bend knees up to make a hill.

line 1 – Starting from ankles, right hand fingers (Jack) and left hand fingers (Jill) walk up legs.

line 2 – Right hand "falls" down hill and then left hand.

INSTRUMENTS "Walk Walk Walk around" can be used with instruments

Play Softly Loudly Quickly Slowly

1. Sing, Play, Sing and Play, Sing and Play together . . .
2. Soft, Soft, play the bells, Softly play together . . .
3. Loud Loud play the drums, Loudly play together . . .
4. Quick Quick play the bells Quickly play together . . .
5. Slow Slow play the drums, Slowly play together . . .

Story Song

LISTENING – There was an old woman   Texas

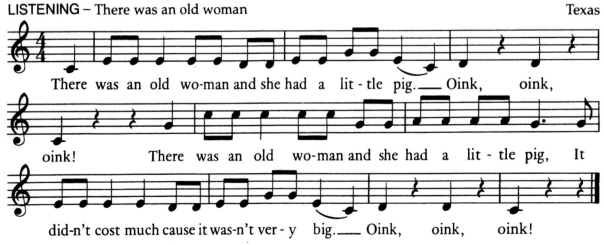

There was an old wo-man and she had a lit - tle pig.___ Oink, oink,

oink! There was an old wo-man and she had a lit - tle pig, It

did-n't cost much cause it was-n't ver - y big.___ Oink, oink, oink!

Five to six years

GENERAL CHARACTERISTICS

Learning

Five year olds are active and eager students who enjoy looking at books and listening to stories about science, space discoveries and the wonders of the world. They are stimulated by short trips in the community and enjoy talking about their adventures. Their attention span is longer and they are ready for a greater variety of activities.

Social development

The five year old is interested in people, what they are doing and where they are going. Social relationships are important and the five year old works and learns well in a group. More individual attention can be given, if groups are not too large − about 12-16 children in a class.

Language

The average five year old may know and use about two thousand words and can repeat or make up quite a long story.

Imagination

Dramatic and imaginative play is a favorite activity. A group of 5 year olds can create and act out a domestic situation, a story, or their interpretation of TV characters. They like to "dress-up," especially if there is a full length mirror in the room. They enjoy creating original movement, rhymes and songs.

DEVELOPING MUSICAL INTEREST

Moving

Five year olds have more body awareness and control. They are ready to use their bodies to feel the elements of music – pulse, rhythm, tempo, rests, dynamics and form, especially if they have learned to listen for musical cues or signals when younger. With these cues, they can start, stop, change tempo, and go forward, backwards or sideways. They can step or clap the beat and rhythm patterns and they probably have learned to "skip". Speech rhythms, rhymes and poems that are spoken, clapped, and stepped, enhance their sense of rhythm.

Singing

The five year old voice is stronger and the sense of pitch will be fairly accurate, if ear and voice have been developed. Research has proved that the young child's natural range is six notes, centering around the F or F# above middle C. Keeping within this range will foster confident and more accurate singing. Traditional singing games, with many repetitions so that each child can have a turn being "it", have the added bonus of "singing practice" (see page 25).

Instruments

Melodic instruments such as tone bars, xylophones and glockenspiels can be used for simple bordun type accompaniments and also for playing short and simple melody patterns. However, these require more technique, and the children must be "ready" – physically and mentally, for the necessary hand-eye co-ordination.

Listening

Sing folk songs or composed songs for the children. Choose records with care. Invite an instrumentalist to visit the class so the children can look closely at the instrument and the player, and also listen to the timbre of the instrument. If the musician can play a song familiar to the children, they will be delighted.

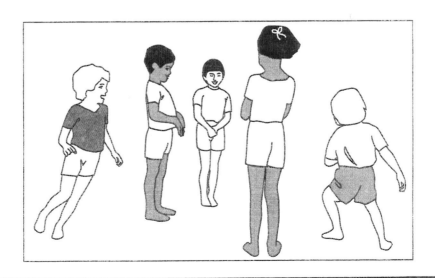

MOVEMENT GAME WITH SPEECH

Step beat feel rest

Doctor Foster went to Gloucester* in a shower of rain (Splash)

He stepped in a puddle right up to his middle

And never went there again. (Turn)

*Pronounced "Gloster"

Speak words clearly and step around the room, all going in the same direction.
Lift knees slightly so children will *step* firmly on the beat.
Clap once on "rest-spaces" with the words "Splash" and "Turn".
On the word "turn", step around in the opposite direction, repeating the rhyme again.

SINGING GAME

Oats, Peas, Beans and Barley grow

Rhythmic drama

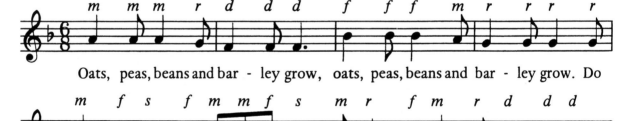

Oats, peas, beans and bar - ley grow, oats, peas, beans and bar - ley grow. Do

you or I or an - y - one know how oats, peas, beans and bar - ley grow?

Verse 1. Stand in your own space; clap on the beat and sing

	(Words)	(Actions)
Verse 2.	First the farmer sows his seed,	– Hold seed in one hand, throw rhythmically with other hand.
	Then he stands and takes his ease,	– Stand, hands on hips
	He stamps his feet and claps his hands	– 2 stamps, 2 claps
	And turns around to view his lands	– Turn in space, 4 steps, shade eyes with hand.
Verse 3.	Walking with a partner	– Find a partner, walk and sing
	Walking with a partner	– Continue to walk and sing with partner
	Make a ring, oh make a ring	– Partners face and hold hands
	Oh while we gaily dance and sing	– Partners circle once.

Repeat game; find a *different* partner in verse 3.

INSTRUMENT GAME

Ensemble

See Saw – Move; Sing; Play

All children, arms outstretched sideways, rock on the beat and sing

Introduction: by teacher on glockenspiel

One child plays alto xylophone and sings

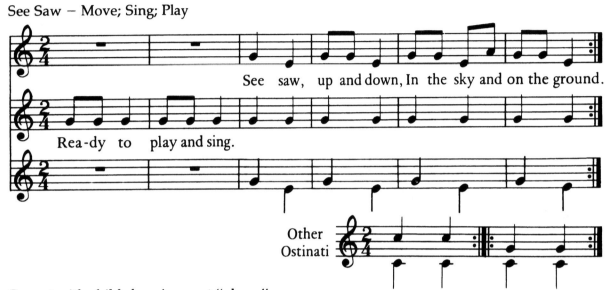

See saw, up and down, In the sky and on the ground.

Rea-dy to play and sing.

Other Ostinati

Repeat with child choosing next "player"

Melody from symphony no. 6 – Beethoven

LISTENING

Words by J.B.

Introducing Beethoven

Ear - ly this morn - ing I heard a ro - bin sing.

He's sing - ing to tell us that soon it will be spring.____

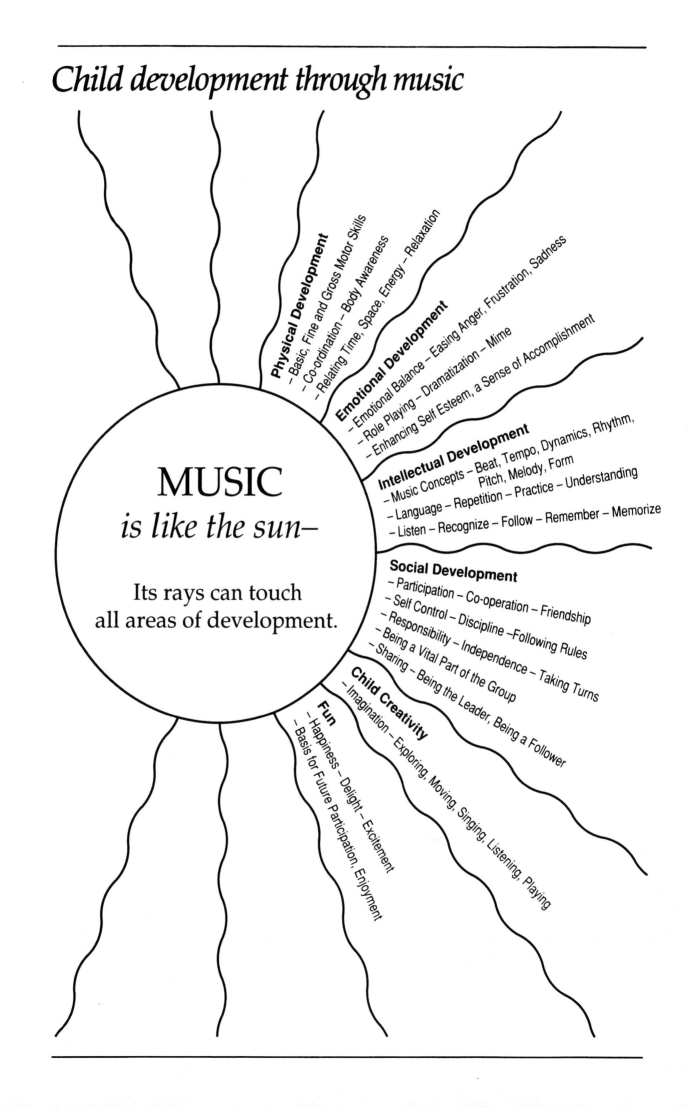

MUSIC
is like the sun–

Its rays can touch
all areas of development.

Physical Development
– Basic, Fine and Gross Motor Skills
– Co-ordination – Body Awareness
– Relating Time, Space, Energy – Relaxation

Emotional Development
– Emotional Balance – Easing Anger, Frustration, Sadness
– Role Playing – Dramatization – Mime
– Enhancing Self Esteem, a Sense of Accomplishment

Intellectual Development
– Music Concepts – Beat, Tempo, Dynamics, Rhythm, Pitch, Melody, Form
– Language – Repetition – Practice – Understanding
– Listen – Recognize – Follow – Remember – Memorize

Social Development
– Participation – Co-operation – Friendship
– Self Control – Discipline –Following Rules
– Responsibility – Independence – Taking Turns
– Being a Vital Part of the Group
– Sharing – Being the Leader, Being a Follower

Child Creativity
– Imagination – Exploring, Moving, Singing, Listening, Playing

Fun
– Happiness – Delight – Excitement
– Basis for Future Participation, Enjoyment

Some words from the child to parent or teacher

1 If you encourage me to move to music (clap, jump, walk, dance, etc.) I will know how music feels. This is my favorite response to music.

2 When I hum or chant unconsciously while I play with my toys, it means that I am feeling good.

3 If you sing to me, then I will learn to sing, too. Repeating favorite songs is never boring, but rather helps me sing better.

4 If you alter a song by putting my name in it, I will know that I am "in" the music. Instead of "Old MacDonald" had a farm, sing "Christopher Harvey had a farm" or Jennifer Shapiro or Taddy Weaver . . .

5 Songs and rhymes with a rhythmic flow of words help me to hear the rhythm of speech and music. It will help my language development, too.

6 If I make up a little song of my own, this creativity is important as a musical experience and to my development as a person.

7 If you and I play games with sounds (animal, machines, "nonsense"), this will interest me in qualities and differences in *sound:* − a short definition − "Music is *sound* and *silence*".

8 I will "turn off" my ears to music if:
   − you try to make me listen to music that is too "grown-up" for me (recordings, radio, concerts, etc.)
   − you try to make me listen to music for longer than my attention span.
   − you play "background" music while I am involved with other activities.

9 If you want to buy me a record, be careful of musical and literary quality, and choose one I can move to or sing with. Passive listening is for older people.

10 If you know a musician who plays an interesting instrument like the cello or the trumpet, I would enjoy an informal visit when I can see, touch and listen to it.

11 Please give me many happy musical experiences before you introduce me to the world of greater music (piano lessons, concerts, choirs, etc.)

12 Remember, you cannot *teach* me to enjoy music but I could *"catch"* it from you.

Further reading

Bruner, J.: **Toward A Theory of Instruction** Harvard University Press, 1971

Cass-Beggs, B.: **Your Child Needs Music** Frederick Harris, 1985
　　　　　　 Your Baby Needs Music Addison Wesley, 1990

Cohen, D. and Stern, V.: **Observing and Recording Behavior** (3rd ed.) Teachers College Press, 1983

Elkind, D.: **The Hurried Child** Addison Wesley, 1981

Fabor, A.; and Mazlich, E.: **How To Talk So Kids Will Listen and Listen So Kids Will Talk** Avon Publishing, 1982

Gardiner, H.: **Frames of Mind, The Theory of Multiple Intelligences** Basic Books, New York, 1983

Hargreaves, D.: **The Developmental Psychology of Music** Cambridge University Press, 1986

McDonald, D. and Simons, G.: **Musical Growth and Development, Birth through Six** Schirmer, 1989

Montessori, M.: **Education for Human Development** Schocken Books, New York, 1976

Moog, H.: **The Musical Experience of the Preschool Child** Trans. Clarke, Schott, 1976

Palmer, M. and Sims, W.: **Music in Pre Kindergarten** M.E.N.C., 1993

Piaget, J.: **The Child's Conception of the World** Littlefield, 1975

Zimmerman, M.: **Musical Characteristics of Children** M.E.N.C., 1971

Student project

Find one other game to develop musical interest in each of the categories – MOVING, SINGING, INSTRUMENTS, LISTENING – for each age group. Then try it with a young child or a group of children. Evaluate your project.

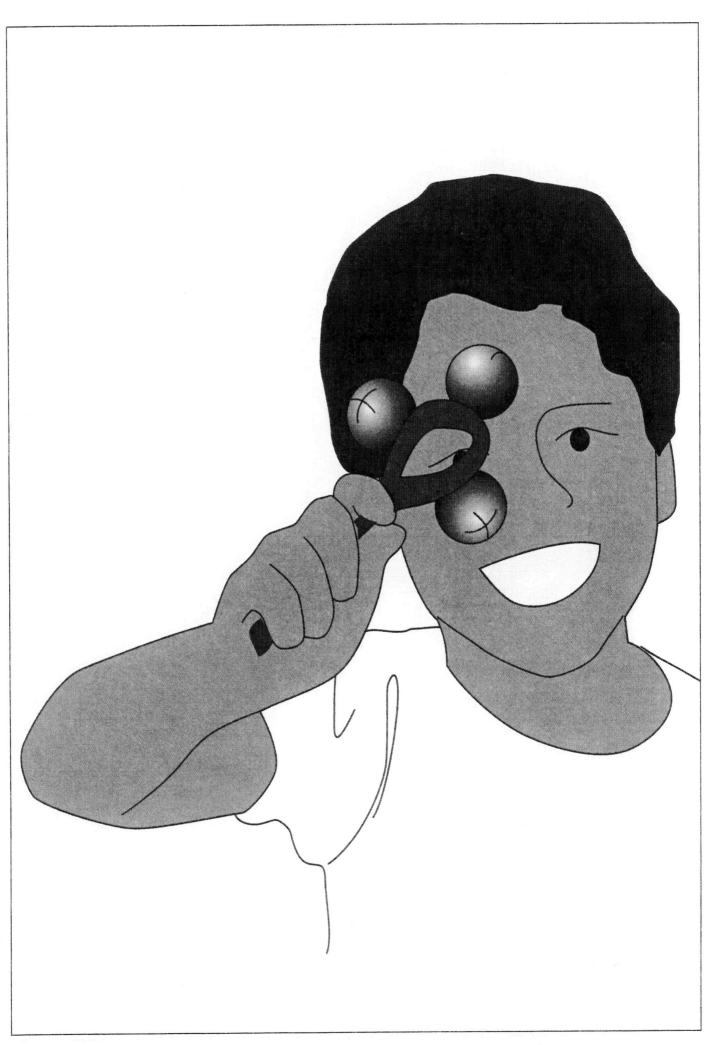

PART II
The Music

Goals of music education in early childhood

Enjoyment & Happiness

Our first and main goal is to encourage every young child to enjoy and be happy with music. Therefore, we must provide a variety of musical experiences at the young child's level of feeling and understanding. The language of music is best learned by starting very early in life.

"The growth of music must be re-enacted in a growing human being and the child must be allowed to go through the various stages starting at the most primitive".

Carl Orff

Preparatory curriculum

We must try to stimulate the young child's natural interest in sound and rhythm with an imaginative and progressive programme. We try to prepare children for the world of greater music by offering happy games where they can subconsciously experience all the elements of music long before we introduce the academic side – ledger lines and dotted eighth notes! Physical and intellectual co-ordination, learning to sing on pitch and intelligent listening are prerequisites to making music on any instrument, so we include these skills in our carefully planned curriculum. Our plans must be relevant to the child's developmental level.

Every child

We must be aware of individual differences, accepting and respecting each child.

We try to develop each child in our care as well as we can. We are very careful of the word "talent". It is too soon to label any child as "talented" or "untalented". *Music is for every child.*

Musical taste

If we are to develop musical taste, we must use music materials of the highest quality. Young children are wide-eyed and open to all things in their environment but they are not mature enough to choose between the good, the mediocre and the bad. The child whose only literary stimulation is "comic books" will not develop good literary taste. "Flashy" wind-up toys give temporary, superficial delight, but they do not have the qualities or possibilities for creative play – like sand, water or blocks. Therefore, when choosing music materials, the teacher must remember that children will "like what they hear". So choose the best.

Listening

Learning to listen is an important ingredient in musical learning. Children in the world of today need special help here. Our sound environment is becoming filled with unpleasant noise – traffic, machines, incessant radio, T.V. and so called "background music" everywhere. Children at a very young age learn to "close their ears" and "turn off" sound. The music teacher must "open ears" and teach children to *listen* to music.

Moving, Singing, Listening, Playing

So with these primary goals in mind, we offer suggestions in four specific activity areas – *Moving, Singing, Listening* and *Playing instruments*. Many activities involve several of the areas, but as young children usually think of one thing at a time, I find it better to organize the work into these four areas. We start in one area and add other activities when the children are ready.

Movement and music
Movement

"Movement is natural and necessary for the child's growth".
Doll and Nelson

Early childhood educators and researchers are aware of the importance of movement education because it makes important contributions to the child's growth and development in the following ways:
1 The development of physical and emotional well-being.
2 The development of a body image and a sense of self.
3 The development of spacial concepts which have to do with
   - *size* - "Jump from the *biggest* block"
   - *shape* - "Walk in a *circle*"
   - *distance* - "Take a *long* step"
   - *area* - "You need a big *space* to twirl"
   - *point of reference* - "Skip away *from the piano*, walk slowly *back to the piano*"
   - *volume* - "Be a pumpkin seed; slowly *grow* into a big pumpkin for Hallowe'en"
   - *balance* - "Stand in the *middle* of the circle" and other spacial ideas.
4 Movement games counteract tension.
5 They build confidence in the withdrawn or insecure child.
6 They develop co-ordination and awareness skills so that the child can move safely among people and things.
7 They stimulate social experiences – the joy of moving in a group, of being a leader or a follower.

"The child's conscious and subconscious movements tell us many things. The child understands much that he cannot yet put into words. He is able, however, to demonstrate these understandings through gestures and other movements. Through careful observation, we can gain some insight into what the child is thinking. Movement thus becomes an important non-verbal tool for learning. Evaluation as to the extent of learning is immediately possible".
Andress-Music Experiences

Music Education and Movement
"Music and movement have separate lives of their own, but in the beginning stages, both can be easily taught together".
Gray and Percival

When movement education is combined with music education, one helps the other – concepts are heightened and clarified for the child. When children are asked to run quickly and then to walk slowly, they are learning to feel two contrasting movement tempi (time). If the quick run is accompanied by quick *sounds*, and the slow walk is accompanied by slow sounds, they are learning to *feel, hear* and *identify* two music tempi. All the basic elements of music can be felt and understood through such music and movement activities – pulse, meter, duration, rhythm patterns, accent, dynamics, melody and form feeling.

Movement education is an important part of the Orff Schulwerk because of its strong emphasis on the rhythmical elements of music. Every lesson in the early stages makes use of the natural movements of children – walking, running, jumping, galloping and skipping – to stimulate listening and quick reaction skills. Simplicity and clarity are stressed, so that *every* child can understand and join the game.
"Elemental music is never music alone but forms a unity with movement, dance and speech".
Carl Orff

Contents of music and movement games

A progressive plan of movement games

For classes of 4, 5 or 6 year old children who are learning to listen.

1 Start and stop

"Walk when I *walk; stop* when I *stop,* you will have to *watch* me".

The teacher walks with the children, at first. All walk around the room in the same direction (counter clockwise works best). The children are learning to pay attention and to move in a group; they are also becoming accustomed to the size and shape of the room and the "feel" of the floor. Encourage all children to participate. Participation is more important than precision in the early stages. Spread out over the whole room. Walking in a line or a symmetrical circle comes later.

2 Follow the sound

"Walk when I *play;* stop when the *sound* stops; you will have to *listen".*

The children walk with the teacher who plays even "walking" sounds on a small hand drum.

Repeat several times, using an 8 bar accompaniment. The children are learning to move and stop with the *sound* of the drum. They are subconsciously feeling the *length* of two phrases. Avoid too much demonstration or verbal explanation. Tell the children *what* to do, not *how* to do it.

When the children are comfortable moving in a group, the teacher should go to the side, to watch *all* the children and help those that require it. At first the teacher should follow the natural tempo and pace of the children with the accompaniment. Change the accompanying *sound* — a pair of rosewood or bamboo sticks, a wood block or the piano give acoustical variety.

Later, change the pace, or tempo, to introduce the concept of *slower* or *faster.* Ask the children to walk in any direction, often turning and changing, *without bumping into anyone.* This requires alertness and good body control.

3 Space games (see Diagrams 1 and 2, page 45)

1 Find your own *space*
2 Stand in your *space*
3 Feel all around your *space* with your arms – do you need to move to a better *space?*
4 Jump in your *space*
5 *Sit* down in your *space* on the floor

In movement classes, children tend to stand too close to each other. A short experience with each of the above "space" games helps them learn the importance of "space". They are then free to move independently in their "own space".

6 Sit on the floor and go round and round in your *space*
7 Sit and go around the other way
8 Kick your feet in your *space*
9 Pat your hands on the floor in your *space*
10 Rock in your space —forwards; backwards; sideways;

Now we are ready for creative, body awareness games.

11 How can you move your *feet* in your space?

12 Think of a *different* way

13 How can you move your legs?

　　Continue with "your arms", your "hands", your "fingers", your "shoulders". What else can you move?

14 What part of your body can you move up and down? (head, foot) forwards and backwards? (hands) open and close? (mouth, eyes, arms)

15 Move *away* from your space on your "seat". Go back and *find* your space.

16 *Crawl* away from your space; now find your space again.

　　Continue with tummy slide, back slide, roll, go backwards, go forwards, go sideways, go slowly, go quickly.

17 Show me another way to go, then come back to your space.

18 Sit on the floor; how could you move if you had no hands? no feet?

4　Animal Walks

Can you walk like a dog? a cat? a bear? a mouse? Choose animals (worms, fish, birds, insects) where the child has seen the *real thing,* if possible. Should we ask young children to "be" animals that they have never seen? Children can add animal *sound effects* to these games.

5　Going places

Be a car; a bus; a motorcycle; a fire engine; a boat; a big truck − with appropriate sounds.

Accompaniment to "space games", "animal walks", and "going places"

At first, do with no accompaniment, then add mouth sounds, percussion or piano improvisations to reflect the qualities (tempo and dynamics) of these movements. This adds a musical dimension to the action; it is also an effective way of controlling the "starting" and the "stopping". Be sure the children understand and can do the "start and stop" game on page 36. Movement requiring 8-16 bars of sounds is long enough at the beginning. Lengthen, as span of attention and skills increase.

6 Help the child develop a *whole body* response to music

Become aware of different parts of the body.

Feel the on-going beat with small repeated actions − clap, pat, tap.

Become aware of personal *space* and the space of others − floor games.

Enjoy participating and being part of a group − singing games.

Develop co-ordination and self-control.

Follow the sound − start . stop . walk . gallop . run . skip − with a musical cue.

Recognize and respond to rhythmic and melodic phrases.

Be ready to invent appropriate actions and sounds in action game songs and in simple drama.

Basic and natural ways for children to move

Walking

Walking helps music. Children can feel the underlying and ongoing pulse and also the concept of the quarter note (♩). This readies them for reading and writing the music symbol.

Music helps walking. It stimulates co-ordination and "flow" of movement.

Walking is a prerequisite to many singing games and dances.

Walking contributes to the child's health and feelings of well-being.

Encourage children to walk well.

Walking Games

1 *Walk around the room while I play the drum (piano)* | | | |
"swing your arms a little – all go the same way around the room – "go into the spaces" – don't bump into anyone". **Stop** when the sound stops.

2 *Walk around the room while I play the drum* | | | |
When you hear a signal, turn and go the other way.

signals   play: ⊓ | ⊓ | or
         say: turn a-round turn a-round   piano

At first, use 8-bar phrase lengths between signals; then change phrase lengths.

3 *Walk and clap*

clap   (a)   (b)   (c)   (d)
walk

Feel the rest with a small, silent hand movement. Keep a steady walking beat.

4 *Walk backwards* while I play the drum (| | | | – slower).
All go the same way – look "over your shoulder" so you won't bump into anyone.

5 *Walk freely, wherever you like*, in the room, while I play the drum – turn and go into the spaces, without bumping anyone.

6 *Walk sideways* – start with your right foot and bring the other foot up beside it. Continue for about 16 bars. Now start with your other foot (left) and go the other way. Accompany with drum, slowly at first.

7 *Step with the beat of the drum*
Lift your knees a little.

      | | | |

Step and say: feel the beat with your feet.

8 *Walk with long steps* – slow tempo accompaniment.
Walk with short steps – faster tempo accompaniment.
Walk with high steps – slower tempo accompaniment.

9 *Walk on your tip toes* – high sound accompaniment (upper register piano, or triangle).

Walk on your heels – low sound accompaniment (lower register piano, or drum).

When I change from high to low, you change (toes to heels).

10 *Speak a rhyme and walk "on the beat"*

   | | | |

Keep in time with a rhyme.

| | | |

Ju-ba this and Ju-ba that

| | | |

Ju-ba has a yellow cat

Find other good "walking rhymes".

11 *Walking in a line*

Choose a leader with a counting out rhyme (see page 75). The leader chooses the second child to stand behind; the second child chooses the third etc. until all children are in the line, with a comfortable space between each child.

Teacher says *starting words* (introduction):

    Ready to walk in line – (drum plays on beat)

Children walk and say:

    Keep in line, keep in line. Everybody keep in line.

    The leader can lead around the outside of the room and then anywhere else, holding one arm or a flag high in the air, so that all can see where to go. Each child should have a turn to be the leader. This prepares the children for other "follow the leader" games.

12 *Walk in a circle – two ways:*

(a) Hold hands and make a circle with me. "Let go hands" and turn with me (teacher makes a *quarter turn* to the right). Allow a moment, with a brief explanation, for children on opposite sides of the circle to realize they will be facing a different way.

Teacher says starting words:

    | | | |

    "Walk in a circle now".

Children and teacher walk and say:

    | | | | | | | ξ

    "Round about and round about and round about we go —

    | | | | | | | |

    Round about and round about, not too fast and not too slow"

(b) Do *not* let go hands this time; turn with me but *still hold hands*. Many traditional circle games are played this way. Five year olds, who are surer of shape formations, are ready to walk in a circle, holding hands. Some teachers make a circle with tape or chalk on the floor, to help the children – with young or handicapped children it may be necessary.

Note: Many "moving circle" games can be simplified by substituting "standing and clapping" for "circling". Accompaniment: At first, the words direct and accompany the movement. Later, variety and interest can be achieved by the teacher using a tambourine, rhythm sticks, a wood block, a bongo drum or piano improvisation to accompany these games.

Galloping games

Galloping is an easy and natural way for young children to move. It is easier than running and much easier than skipping. Show the children how to put one foot forward and keep that *same* foot in *front* all through the galloping. Next, try putting the other foot "first" and keeping it in front. A wood block or rhythm sticks make a good accompaniment ♩ ♪♩ ♪ for galloping.

1 Walking games 1, 2, 5 and 6 work well with galloping.

2 Horse or pony game

Gallop like a frisky horse (lift knees).

Gallop like a tired horse (slower and slower).

Gallop like a big, slow horse (heavy, slow walk).

Gallop like a small, quick pony (quick gallop with small steps).

Each kind of horse will need a different tempo and different dynamics in the accompaniment — staccato, legato, heavily, lightly.

Running games

Children require co-ordination and quick reaction skills to run in a group. I have observed that children are running with more skill and style at present, perhaps influenced by the adult jogging "craze". Encourage light running, with the children using the ball of the foot, not the *whole foot*, and taking *small* steps. The concept of eighth notes (⊓ ⊓) can be introduced through running.

1 Walking games 1, 2, 4, 5, 8 and 11 also make good running games, provided the children are ready for these activities. **Running and listening in a group requires skill and control.**

2 Run and fall down

This is fun, and also teaches the children "how to fall" safely. Stand in your space; hold your arms straight down in front of you with the front (palms) of your hands facing the floor. Run when the drum tells you to run ♩♩ ♩♩ When it stops ♩ use your hands to help you "fall" down on the floor. Run again when the drum tells you. Repeat a number of times, with a different length of time between each "fall".

3 Run and make a statue (freeze).

The same as game 2, but ask the child to make a *different statue* each time the drum stops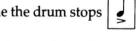

4 Follow the drum

The drum "walks" and "runs" alternately. The children must listen and control their bodies for this excellent game. They are, subconsciously, beginning to feel ♩ and ♩♩.

Jumping games

Show children how to jump on the *ball* of the foot and how to bend their knees with a little "spring". Accompaniment ♩ ♩ ♩ ♩

1 Jump in your space.

2 Turn around while you jump; now, go the other way.

3 Make a big slow jump. ♩ ♩ ♩ ♩

4 Make a small, quick jump. ♫ ♫ ♫ ♫ ♫

5 Bounce like a ball when the sound *jumps* on the tambourine.

About 8 bars of each action at first, then vary length.

Hopping games

These prepare the children for "skipping".

    1 Can you *stand* on one foot? Can you *hop* on one foot?

    2 Can you *stand* on the other foot? Can you *hop* on the other foot?

    3 Hop 4 times on one foot, then 4 times on the other foot.

    4 Repeat, hopping 3 times, then twice, then *once* on each foot.

This could be the beginning of "skipping".

Skipping games

Introduce skipping when the children are about four and a half or five. Some skip sooner and some later, but be ready with some tactful help and encouraging words. The child often views skipping as an important accomplishment.

Accompanying rhythm pattern is ♩. ♪ ♩. ♪ or ♩ ♩ ♪ ♪

1 Walking games 1, 2, 4, 5 and 11 work well with skipping.

2 Skipping tag game

    a) Make a circle; drop hands; all take two long steps backwards to make a larger circle; all *sit* down in this new space. All hold one hand out, *palm up*.

    b) Teacher touches palms of children, around circle, chanting a counting out game, to find "it" (see page 75)

    c) "It" skips around inside circle to skipping music on drum or piano.

    d) "It" touches one of the sitting children on the hand and then skips away; the second child rises and chases (skipping) the first child, trying to touch "it" on the back. If successful, *first child rejoins the circle, putting both hands behind back so *all* will know who has had a turn. The second child becomes the new "it". If the child cannot catch "it", the teacher can tactfully end the chase by stopping the accompaniment and preceeding from *

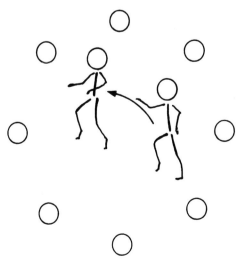

Skipping tag keeps quite a large group of children interested in watching the "chase". It motivates children to practice "skipping".

Rule: Running is *not* permitted in this game.

Combining rhythms

1 What does the drum (or music) say?

Play excerpts (8-10 bars) of:

walking 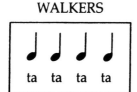 , running  , or skipping

The children listen and then do what the drum "says".

Change the order of the rhythms; the accompanying instrument; the melody (if you are using the piano).

2 Divide class into three groups: "the walkers", "the skippers" and "the runners". Each group goes to its own house (corner).

"Stay in *your* house until you hear *your* music"

"When you hear *your* music, come out and show us *who* you are".

To introduce symbol reading ( ) a leader from each group can carry a symbol sign (5-6 year olds)

WALKERS	RUNNERS	SKIPPERS
ta ta ta ta	ti ti ti ti ti ti ti ti	ta ti ta ti ta ti ta ti

Thus the children learn to *read* and *understand* the symbols. Then, they could learn to *write* these symbols on a blackboard or a plain piece of paper (staff lines are not necessary until melody is introduced). Five and six year olds enjoy "writing music" but be sure they have many experiences with the game, first. *Duration sounds and symbols* can also be learned, now, while clapping the rhythm (see page 184).

3 Slow walk; step wait game

Take a short step forward with one foot. *Wait* on that foot while touching the toe of the *other* foot on the floor, *behind*. Continue, evenly and slowly, with alternate feet stepping forward. The children can say "step wait" as they do this.

The drum or piano plays

step wait   step wait   step wait   step wait

ta-a ta-a ta-a ta-a

The children are, subconsciously feeling "half notes" . When they have practised and learned to keep their balance in this game, add it to the previous game.

Suggestions:

Prepare a "pretend" candle for each child with a 12" cardboard tube topped with a yellow tennis ball. Demonstrate the stately dignified walk for a procession. Each child practices the technique, then all can walk slowly while the adult plays/sings this beautiful melody.

Choral

Robert Schumann

Smoothly, slow walk, holding a make-believe candle

Slow tempo

Walk - ing slow - ly with my can - dle,

Step step step step step step step step

Walk - ing slow - ly in the — night.

step step step step step step stop.

Walk - ing slow - ly with my can - dle,

Step step step step step step step step

Walk - ing slow - ly in the — night.

step step step step step step stop.

Improvisation and creativity

In early childhood education, the creative activities of art, music and play are as important as any other part of the curriculum. We give young children many opportunities to choose activities and materials where they can express their own ideas, feelings and thoughts e.g. paint, clay, paper, sand, blocks. These opportunities should also be available to the child in music through movement, speech, song and percussion instruments. There are many areas of the child's life where we cannot give this freedom, so improvisation and creativity are doubly important to the child's development as a person. In every music class, each child should have opportunities to make suggestions, develop an idea, solve a problem, or show the class a different way of doing an activity. Movement is a natural activity for the beginnings of improvisation where children can experience the joy of self-expression and can develop a growing confidence in themselves as creators.

Space games p. 36, animal walks p. 37, going places p. 37, and role-playing games p. 50 offer the child such opportunities. The teacher provides a "framework" and then *asks the child* what to do, or how to do it. Give *every* child an opportunity to make a suggestion or show it to the group. "Leslie, what kind of an animal (machine, bird, insect) would you like to be today? Show us. Now we can all try".

Structured movement and singing games

The actions of these games follow the words of the game song. This makes them suitable for the young child. Each time the game is repeated, usually many times, the action follows a similar pattern. The child knows what will happen next and this gives confidence to a new or insecure child. Also, the repetition helps develop the singing skills of the child. And, a group activity game helps the child to know what it is like to be a member of a group, without losing feelings of individuality.

Structured games are also easier for the teacher, because the words of the game — song tell the children what to do, so few verbal explanations are necessary. Also these words are a "built-in" control; this is helpful with large groups, new groups, parties or programmes for parents. Every teacher should have a repertoire of structured movement games, including traditional finger plays, singing games, play-party games and folk dances.

Traditional singing games are a part of our culture and should be passed on to all children, as part of growing up. Some traditional games must be adapted for young children, but try to keep the essential quality and spirit of the original game. "The farmer's in the dell" is traditionally played with a circle of moving children, holding hands. This is difficult or impossible for four year olds. In the next section "A teaching sequence for games", this circling procedure comes well down on the list. See page 121 for a 3-4 year old version of "The farmer's in the dell".

A pedagogical sequence for structured games

This must be carefully worked out by each teacher so that first games match the maturity and the abilities of the children – *start where the child is*. Skills learned in first games should prepare children for more challenging games.

The First Stage
1. Space Games
Free formation games are in random spaces, dependent on the floor space – they stimulate space concepts and body awareness. *Sit or stand in your own space. More your arms around you. Find a better space if you are touching someone.*

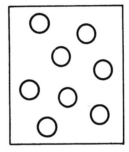

Some examples: Space games 36, Winter games 56, Point to the ceiling 131, Finger play rhymes, Andy Pandy 73, Teddy Bear 98, See Saw 92

This Little Puffin by E. Matterson has many other examples of traditional finger play games.

2. Move away – find your space again
The children learn to move in a class environment without bumping. They are becoming aware of spacial relationships and simple directionality. Whole body movement with large muscle development are encouraged.

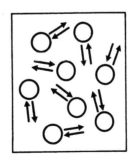

Some examples: crawl, roll, wriggle away from your space – can you find your space again? Space games 36, Animal walks 37, Going places 37, Roll my ball 59, Hop old squirrel 102, All the little ducklings 108, See the ponies 125

Young children should have some days, weeks or months of these first games before trying games that require more structured formation. The teacher sings the words and controls the movement with instrumental and/or vocal accompaniment.

The Second Stage – Circle Games

1. *Sitting or standing circle games*. Young children do not naturally play in a circle. Allow time to teach them to make a circle and then to *sit* or *stand* with good spacing. Then all can see the teacher and each other. All do the same actions led by the teacher. The children are learning to pay attention, watch carefully and imitate the leader.

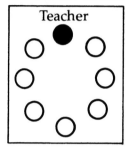

Some examples – Finger plays and "whole body" plays, work well in a sitting or standing circle. Tommy Thumb 124, Star light 93, Rain Rain 92, Bye Baby Bunting 93, I love little pussy 116, I see the moon 99, Looby loo 122, Fuzzy Wuzzy 106

2. *Circle game with "it" in the middle*. One child has a special leading role to play. The children must learn to wait for a turn to be the leader – and be ready to take that responsibility willingly and happily. The child is learning to be a *follower* or a *leader* in the middle of the circle.

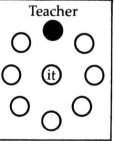

Some examples: Here sits a monkey 105, Hop old squirrel 102, Jack be nimble 94, Punchinello 109, The farmer's in the dell 121, Who's that knocking 114, Five little robins 120 is a *line game* for this stage.

3. *Circle game with one or more children moving behind, in front of, or between the other children*. Moving child must choose another child at the right moment in the music. The children acquire a better sense of direction, know the correct moment for particular action and are able to do it.

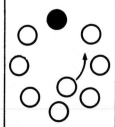

Examples: Lucy 96, Charlie 97, A bluebird 104, Skipping Tag 41, Mary had a 100, The closet key 103, Skip one window 110, I sent a letter 117

The Third Stage – Partner, Moving Circle and Line Games

These games require movement and listening skills, body coordination, cooperation with a partner and/or the group, and a longer attention span.

1. *Partner games.* Walk with a friend. The child learns how to coordinate actions and cooperate with another child.

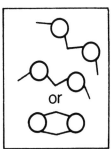

   Some examples: Partner games 53, Ring around a rosie 101, Pat a cake 9, Row your boat 53, Oats, peas beans 24.

2. *Moving circle with the children holding hands.* Teach children to turn bodies slightly in the direction they are going. Teach them to stay in a neat circle and to step together (on the beat, more or less). The children learn to move in a group circle formation and sing all the words throughout the game.

   Some examples: All around the buttercup 112, Sally go 'round the sun 113.

3. *Moving circle with children* not *holding hands.* Teach the children to step around together, on the beat. Teach them to keep a neat circle formation and be aware of the space between each other. These games *fine tune* a feeling for space, pace and directionality while the children sing or say all the words.

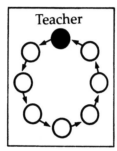

Some examples: The Grande old Duke of York 66, Doctor Foster 24.

4. *Moving a line with a leader.* (a) Make a line as suggested on page 39. The teacher is the leader, first. Tell the children that "we are *not* going in a circle – we will go across the room, along the wall and maybe into the corners." Later, each child, in turn, can be the leader, with the former leader going to the end of the line. Later, "drop hands" and change to galloping or skipping in a line, adding different arm movements or clapping.

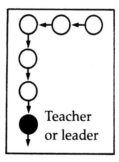

Some examples: Let's take a walk 111, Engine Engine 95, Down the road 111.

The fourth stage for 6-8 year olds.

1. *Two moving circles.* One circle goes counter clockwise and the other clockwise.

   These games continue to develop the importance of spacing, direction and a circle that can get larger or smaller as the game progresses.

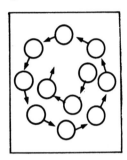

   An example: Down came a lady 118.

2. *Walking with a partner around the circle:* The children must have a happy/good feeling for cooperation, directionality and knowing exactly when to do the correct action as they sing.

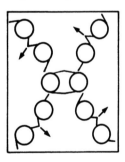

   An example: Here we go 'round the mountain 119.

3. *Two lines: partners face each other.* One pair walks down and back between the lines. They must know the moment in the music to turn, go the other way, and find their new place.

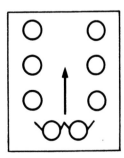

   An example: The big ship sails 123.

   And now you are all ready to join your local "line" or "square dance" group!

Role playing movement games with suggested accompaniment

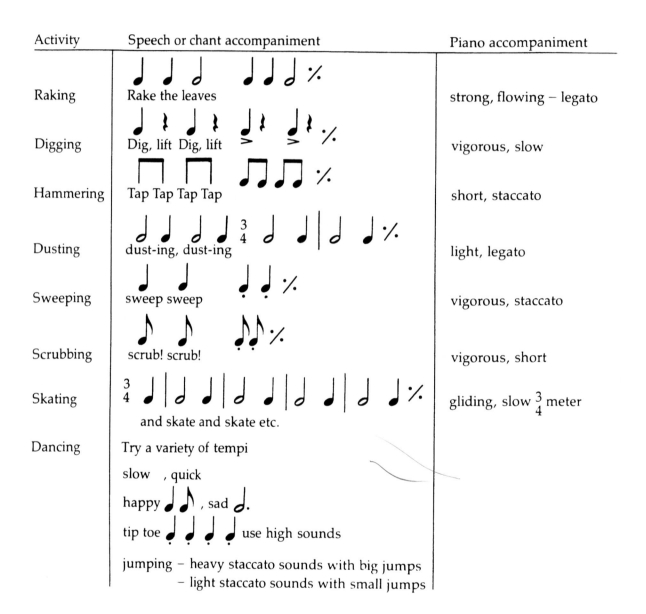

Activity	Speech or chant accompaniment	Piano accompaniment
Raking	Rake the leaves	strong, flowing – legato
Digging	Dig, lift Dig, lift	vigorous, slow
Hammering	Tap Tap Tap Tap	short, staccato
Dusting	dust-ing, dust-ing	light, legato
Sweeping	sweep sweep	vigorous, staccato
Scrubbing	scrub! scrub!	vigorous, short
Skating	and skate and skate etc.	gliding, slow $\frac{3}{4}$ meter
Dancing	Try a variety of tempi slow , quick happy , sad tip toe use high sounds jumping – heavy staccato sounds with big jumps – light staccato sounds with small jumps	

Accompaniments

1 Body sounds with voice (clap and chant).
2 Piano accompaniment for those who can improvise.
3 No accompaniment, to encourage "inner-hearing".
4 Vary sound level; soft sounds encourage children to listen.
5 Children can accompany their dancing with jingles, maracas or hand drums.
6 Teachers and children will become more aware of the differences in sound accompaniments through role playing games and dancing.

Relaxation games

ctive participation is exciting and fun for the children but they tire easily. Moments of quiet physical and mental relaxation prepare body and mind for future learning. Every music class should have one or two *short* rest periods. Resting "stories" suggest an activity that leads to rest. Speak in a quiet voice.

1 Be a tree – hold your arms up like branches – the wind shakes the leaves – the leaves fall down slowly, slowly and lie on the ground . . . . .

2 The rabbits are hopping in the forest – soon they are tired and need a rest – crawl into your den and go to sleep . . . . .

3 Lie on your back – rest your arms – rest your legs – rest your fingers – rest your head – rest your eyes . . . . .

4 Be a rag doll, lying on the floor – I will come and feel your arm (or leg) to see if it is loose and floppy – (quietly move to *each* child and "test" arms or legs).

5 Sing a quiet resting song or lullaby to the children.

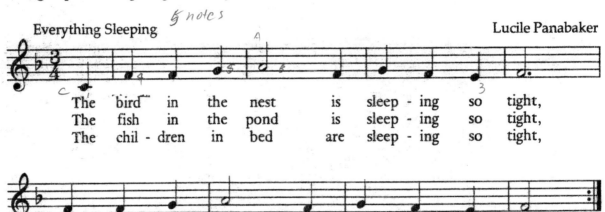

Everything Sleeping   Lucile Panabaker

The bird in the nest is sleep - ing so tight,
The fish in the pond is sleep - ing so tight,
The chil - dren in bed are sleep - ing so tight,

ev - ery thing sleep - ing, All through the night.

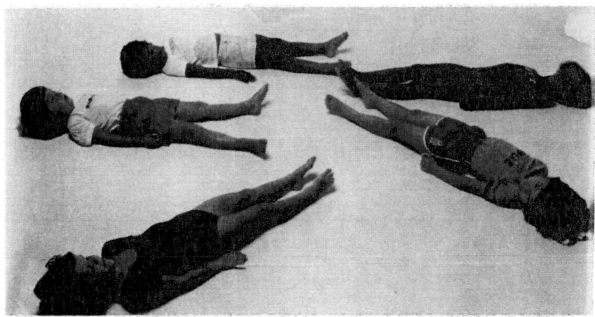

51

More lullabies

1 The parent sings to the child. Substitute the name of your child in these lullabies.
2 The teacher sings to the resting children.
3 The children sing and rock "pretend" or real dolls.

1. Mammy Loves

Mam - my loves and pap - py loves and Mam - my loves her ba - by.

Go to sleep now, go to sleep, go to sleep you lit - tle ba - by.

2. Hush Little Baby

Hush lit - tle ba - by don't say a word, Mom - ma's going to

buy you a mock - ing bird It can whi - stle and

it can sing, It can do most an - y - thing.

3. Fais do - do

Fais do do, Co-las mon p'tit frère, — Fais do do, t'au-ras du lo - lo. Ma-
  Ro-bert
Ma-rie ma p'tite soeur, —

man est en haut Qui fait du ga-teau, Pa-pa est en bas qui fait du cho-co-lat,

Fais do do, Co-las, mon p'tit frère — Fais do do, t'au-ras du lo - lo.

Movement games to teach the elements of music

This section is for older children (5-8).

The teacher should understand the musical concept being taught.

1 Partner Games. The children should have several months of individual movement games before trying partner games. It takes time to feel comfortable when holding another child's hand and to develop the coordination and cooperation needed. These games are a valuable preparation for "moving" circle games.

Rhythm

a) *Walk* with a partner when I play ♩ ♩ ♩ ♩ (drum, piano)

Skip by yourself when I play ♩ ♪♩ ♪♩ ♪♩ ♪ (about 8 bars of each)
The music will tell you what to do. Find your own partner (after skipping). Next time, find a different partner.

Beat

b) *Face* your partner

1 Clap your own hands, slowly
2 Pat your partner's hands slowly; and now combine

       | | | |
Teacher: Ready to clap   pat (introduction, to set the beat)

       | | | | | | |
Children: Clap pat clap pat clap pat stop

Beat

c) "Ring around a rosy" for partners. Sing and play traditional game. Walk around on a slow beat. When you "fall down" be ready to get up and play it again *or* play another game on the floor.

Slow beat

d) "Row, row, row your boat" for partners.

Sit on the floor, with one child's knees on top of the other child's knees (legs outstretched). Sing traditional song, and rock back and forth on the beat, slowly. Children learn to cooperate with each other and synchronize their rocking in this game.

Traditional

Row, row, row your boat, Gent-ly down the stream,
Merr-i-ly, merr-i-ly, merr-i-ly, merr-i-ly, Life is but a dream.

Meter,
Anacrusis,
Rhythm

2 Rhythm Walks.

(a) Skate and twirl

Skate (slide) with long gliding steps;

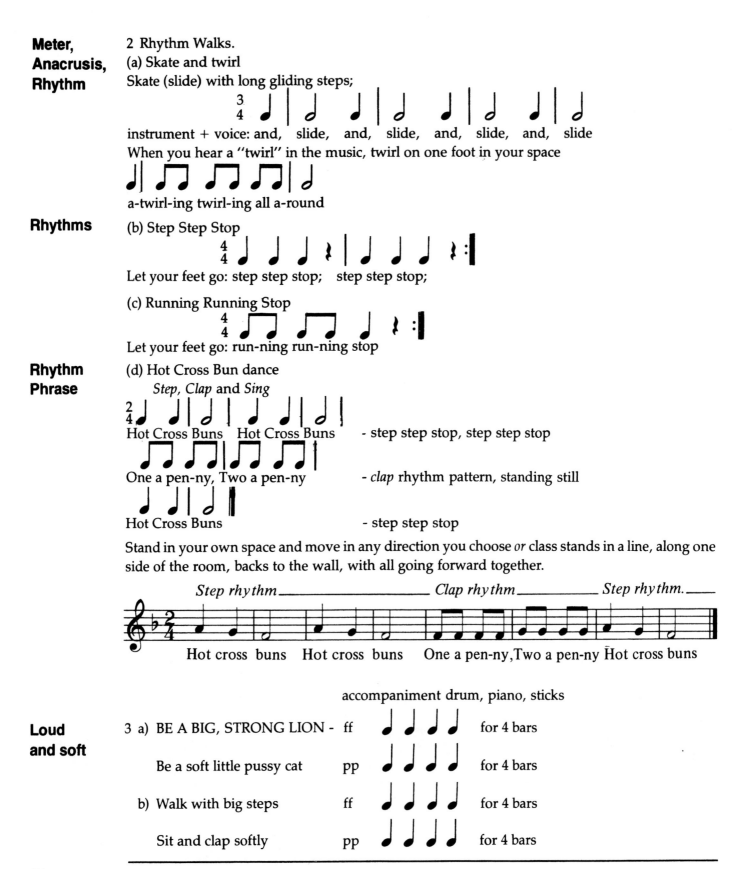

instrument + voice: and, slide, and, slide, and, slide, and, slide

When you hear a "twirl" in the music, twirl on one foot in your space

a-twirl-ing twirl-ing all a-round

Rhythms

(b) Step Step Stop

Let your feet go: step step stop; step step stop;

(c) Running Running Stop

Let your feet go: run-ning run-ning stop

Rhythm
Phrase

(d) Hot Cross Bun dance

Step, Clap and Sing

Hot Cross Buns   Hot Cross Buns   - step step stop, step step stop

One a pen-ny, Two a pen-ny   - *clap* rhythm pattern, standing still

Hot Cross Buns   - step step stop

Stand in your own space and move in any direction you choose *or* class stands in a line, along one side of the room, backs to the wall, with all going forward together.

*Step rhythm*_____ *Clap rhythm*_____ *Step rhythm.*_____

Hot cross buns   Hot cross buns   One a pen-ny, Two a pen-ny Hot cross buns

accompaniment drum, piano, sticks

Loud
and soft

3 a) BE A BIG, STRONG LION - ff   for 4 bars

Be a soft little pussy cat   pp   for 4 bars

b) Walk with big steps   ff   for 4 bars

Sit and clap softly   pp   for 4 bars

**Fast
and slow**

accompaniment drum, piano, sticks

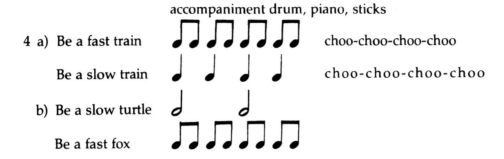

4 a) Be a fast train   choo-choo-choo-choo

    Be a slow train   choo-choo-choo-choo

    b) Be a slow turtle

    Be a fast fox

**High
and low**

5 Preparation:
  Play some high, slow sounds on the treble end of piano.
  Tell the children "these are high sounds".
  Play some low, slow sounds on the bass end of piano.
  Tell the children "these are low sounds".
  Game:
  a) When I play skipping sounds ♩♪♩♪ ♪♩♩♪ , go skipping in the park
     When I play a high sound − be a tree.
     When I play a low sound − be a flower.
  b) When I play high sounds, fly like a bird.
     When I play low sounds, crawl like a snake.

**High,
middle
and low**

6 a) Play some sounds near the middle of the piano. "These are sounds in the middle". Review
    "high" and "low" sounds. Add the middle idea to the above games. "When I play sounds in
    the middle, be a bush", in 5a. When I play sounds in the middle, be yourself, walking, in 5b.
  b) When I play high sounds, pat your head
    When I play middle sounds, pat your tummy
    When I play low sounds, pat your feet
    Change order and phrase lengths in games 5 and 6 to see if the children really understand this
    concept.

**Ascending,
Descending**

7 Melody going higher and lower
  Stand with your back to the wall
  When the melody goes higher, walk forward on the beat.
  When the melody goes lower, walk backward on the beat.
  When the melody stays the same, mark time in one place.
  − an arpeggio melody, with wider intervals going higher and lower, could be played at first,
  and then, later, a scale-type melody. Use the piano or a xylophone with a slow even walking
  tempo.

Accent

8 A sudden loud sound.

The Hallowe'en ghost walk

Walk quietly anywhere you like, in the room. The teacher plays quiet walking music on piano or xylophone. When you hear a sudden loud sound, say "Booh!" Continue with longer and shorter phrase lengths for the quiet ghost walking.

Meter
2 3 4 5
4, 4, 4, 4

9 Play games to give the child the *feeling* of meter before counting beats. These require piano improvisations in the proper meter with an accent on the first beat of the bar.

a) Winter games with suggested piano improvisations.

D. J. W.

Chop Ice

$\frac{2}{4}$ *Say or Sing:*

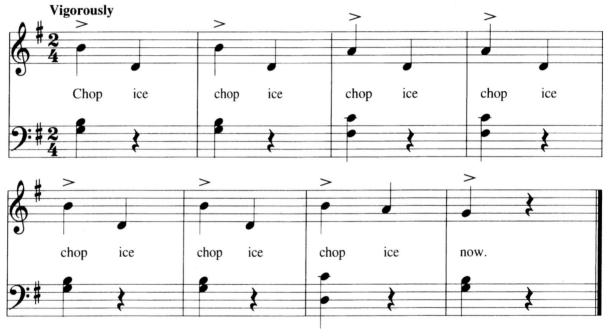

Chop ice chop ice chop ice chop ice

chop ice chop ice chop ice now.

Snowman Dance

$\frac{3}{4}$ *Say or Sing:*

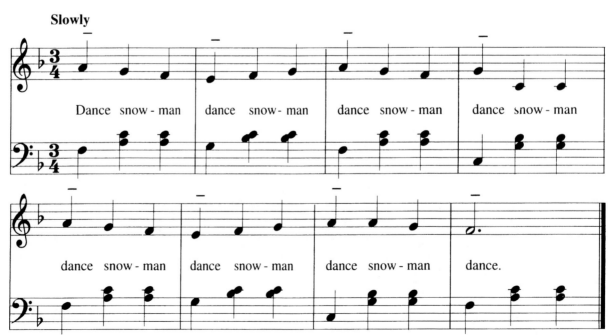

Dance snow-man dance snow-man dance snow-man dance snow-man

dance snow-man dance snow-man dance snow-man dance.

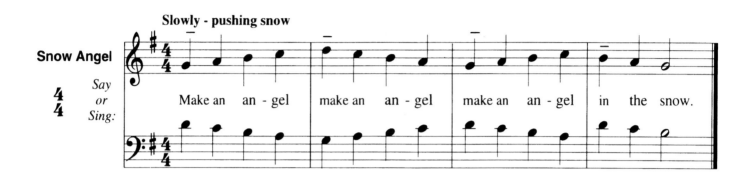

Snow Angel

Slowly - pushing snow

⁴⁄₄ *Say or Sing:* Make an an - gel make an an - gel make an an - gel in the snow.

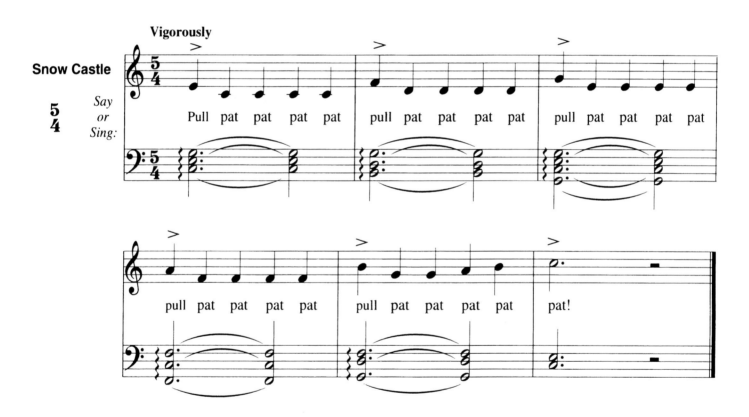

Snow Castle

Vigorously

⁵⁄₄ *Say or Sing:* Pull pat pat pat pat pull pat pat pat pat pull pat pat pat pat

pull pat pat pat pat pull pat pat pat pat pat!

b) ²⁄₄ Step wait

Step forward with one foot on first beat, point toe of other foot *behind,* on second beat

Piano improvisation

²⁄₄			./.
step	point		

³⁄₄ step wait wait

Step forward with one foot on first beat, point toe of other foot *twice,* behind, on second and third beat.

Piano improvisation

³⁄₄				./.
step	point	point		

c) $\frac{2}{4}$ with a ball – bounce, catch, for 8 bars. Piano improvisation | $\frac{2}{4}$ | | `/.` bounce catch |

$\frac{3}{4}$ with a ball – bounce, catch, wait, for 8 bars.

Piano improvisation | $\frac{3}{4}$ | | | `/.` bounce catch wait |

Form or design

10 a) Phrase feeling

Children stand in a **large** circle. The actions should clearly reflect the four different phrases.

Frère Jacques   French

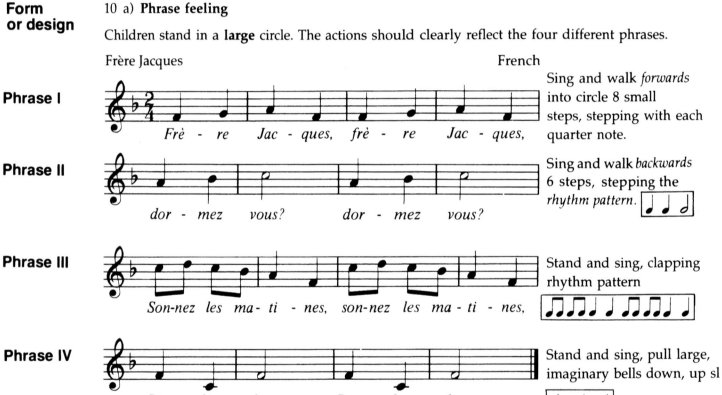

Phrase I
Frè - re   Jac - ques,   frè - re   Jac - ques,
Sing and walk *forwards* into circle 8 small steps, stepping with each quarter note.

Phrase II
dor - mez   vous?   dor - mez   vous?
Sing and walk *backwards* 6 steps, stepping the *rhythm pattern.*

Phrase III
Son-nez les ma- ti - nes,   son-nez les ma - ti - nes,
Stand and sing, clapping rhythm pattern

Phrase IV
Din   dan   don.   Din   dan   don.
Stand and sing, pull large, imaginary bells down, up sl

Children stand in a *large* circle. The actions should clearly reflect the four different phrases.

b) Another game song with two distinct sections (Binary or A. B.) e.g., Here we go Looby Loo page 122
Part I (chorus) clap
Part II (verse) hands, feet etc. "in" and "out"

c) Game songs with three distinct sections (Ternary or A.B.A.)

Roll my ball/En roulant

French Canadian (English text by E. Buttolph)
French adaption by Claire Bellinger

A

Roll my ball, go rol-ling a - long, roll my ball, go rol - ling.
En rou-lant, ma boule_ rou-lant, En rou-lant, ma bou - le.

Turn - ing o - ver, o - ver a - gain, roll my ball, go rol - ling.
En rou-lant, ma bou-lant rou-lant, En rou-lant, ma bou - le.

B

Now I'm going to bounce you, now I'm going to bounce you.
Bou - le sau - te sau - te, Saute en - core et se re-pose.

Bounc-ing, bounc-ing, on your toes, that's the way the rub-ber ball goes.
Sau - te, sau - te, sau - te, saute, sau - te, sau - te, sau - te, saute.

A

Roll my ball, go rol-ling a - long, roll my ball, go rol - ling.
En rou-lant, ma boule_ rou-lant, En rou-lant, ma bou - le.

Turn - ing o - ver, o - ver a - gain, roll my ball, go rol - ling.
En rou-lant, ma bou-lant rou-lant, En rou-lant, ma bou - le.

Teacher sings. Children are balls, rolling on the floor

A   Children roll on the floor; change direction at bar 5 (new phrase)

B   Children stand and bounce (jump, bending knees) Hold last note "goes", until all children are back lying on the floor

A   Repeat 1st part, rolling like balls.

When the children are very familiar with the game, ask them to sit and sing the song while the *teacher listens.*

d) Rondo with movement

In rondo form, the main theme alternates with several contrasting themes.

In this rondo, the main theme is A and the contrasting themes are B and C.
The complete plan is A. B. A. C. A.

Proceed immediately from one theme to the next. The half note at the end of each theme is a clear signal for the children, and a musical way to end each theme.

The accompaniment requires skill to go smoothly from one theme to the next
Drum or Piano: A walk, B gallop, C run, improvization.
Piano A-Baa Baa Blacksheep, B-Pop goes the weasel, C-Polly put the Kettle On.

e) The Eight Game – a Movement Canon (5+) for children with some music experience – When the class has mastered the *Movement Rondo*, try the **Eight Game** with 4 consecutive movement activities:

A. Walk 8 Steps, exactly
B. Stand, Clap 8 Claps, exactly
C. Skip 8 Skips, exactly
D. Kneel on one knee, Count 8 beats "inside"
   Repeat once, ending on D (Kneel)

The children learn to think ahead and be ready for the next movement activity – an important skill in music performance. When they can do this with confidence, divide the group in half, the ONE's and the TWO's. Ask each group to stand at opposite sides of the room, with a leader for each group. Briefly describe a canon or round to the children where the ONE's walk in phrase A and the TWO's stand still. The ONE's Clap B while the TWO's Walk A. Continue the sequence with C and D. Repeat the sequence A B C D once more, ending with ONE's kneeling on one knee. They wait there while the TWO's continue the sequence with C and then join the ONE's on their knees for D. Here is a diagram of this canon.

Canon	ONE's	A	B	C	D	A	B	C	D____	
plan	TWO's		A	B	C	D	A	B	C	D

The Little Brown Tulip Bulb

A movement drama for Spring (4-6 years of age)

Story Teller (Teacher)

Out in my garden, there's a little brown tulip bulb
Sound asleep under all the ice and snow

Ask one or several children to be tulip bulbs. They curl up on the centre of the floor and go to sleep. The other children stand on the side, ready to be the *wind*, the *rain*, or the *sun*.
Music: 4 bars of soft sleeping music on alto xylophone or piano.

One day the wind came from the sky
And blew all over the garden.

The *wind children*, with flapping arms, walk or run around the garden, making wind sounds "ooooh".
Music: 4 bars of wind – sounds (glissandos) on xylophone or piano.

The wind goes to the tulip bulb's door, knocks and says, "WAKE UP TULIP BULB. IT'S SPRING!".

But the tulip bulb says in a slow, sleepy voice, "I'M TOO TIRED" and goes back to sleep.
The wind goes back to its home in the sky.

Another day, the rain came from the sky
And rained all over the garden

The *rain children*, with "dripping" arms, walk or run around the garden, chanting drip-drop sounds.
Music: 4 bars "drip drop" sounds on xylophone or piano.

The rain goes to the tulip bulb's door, knocks and says, "WAKE UP TULIP BULB. IT'S SPRING!".
But the tulip bulb says in a slow, sleepy voice, "I'M TOO TIRED" and goes back to sleep.
The rain goes back to its home in the sky.

Another day, the sun came from the sky,
And shone all over the garden.

The *sun children* make a big sun with their arms, shine (smile) and walk slowly around the garden, making *no* sound.
Music: 4 bars of one soft high repeated sound on xylophone or piano.

The sun goes to the tulip bulb's door, knocks, and says, "WAKE UP TULIP BULB. IT'S SPRING!".
But the tulip bulb says in a slow, sleepy voice, "I'M TOO TIRED" and goes back to sleep.
The sun goes back to its home in the sky.

How can we wake up the sleepy tulip bulb???

One spring day, the <u>wind</u> and the <u>rain</u> and the <u>sun</u> all came to the garden together.

The *wind, rain* and *sun* children move around the garden.
Music: a short sequence of wind, rain and sun music on xylophone or piano.

They all go to the tulip bulb's door, knock and say "WAKE UP TULIP BULB. IT'S SPRING!".
They made so much noise that the tulip bulb couldn't stay asleep any longer.

The *wind, rain,* and *sun* children sit on the floor and watch as the tulip bulb slowly grows taller and taller.

And the tulip bulb slowly grew into a beautiful tulip flower.

Music: arpeggio melody, starting *lower* and growing *higher* on xylophone or piano.

Out in my Garden, there is a beautiful, beautiful tulip flower.

Note:

The Tulip Bulb movement drama and many other movement games in this text are shown with children's classes on a 30 minute VHS video *MOVING TO THE MUSIC* produced and available from: **Video Variables, 864 Millwood Road., Toronto, Ontario, M4G 1W6, Telephone: (416) 423-0077**

Music and Movement Classes

Ten practical suggestions

1 Organize children into groups of eight to sixteen children. The number will depend on physical and cognitive development of the children, and their experience. A teacher with little experience would be wise to start with a small group.

2 Because of physical differences and rapid growth during the early years, the age *span* in each group should be about six to eight *months,* if possible.

3 The movement room should be about 20 feet by 30 feet. It should be pleasant and well lighted with good ventilation. *There should be as little extraneous furniture or equipment as possible.* Cloakroom, changing room and a bathroom should be adjacent.

4 The floor must be clean and smooth but not slippery (e.g. wood, mastic tile, linoleum). Carpet may inhibit some floor movement and is harder to clean; but it may correct poor acoustics.

5 The children should be dressed for action. Tee shirts with shorts or longer pants and rubber soled shoes are satisfactory in the nursery school or kindergarten. The ideal movement costume is a short body suit (leotard) for girls and a pair of gym shorts for boys. I recommend bare legs and bare feet for freedom and safety. Some teachers prefer flexible pull-on slippers available at dance supply stores. Jewellry, toys and extra sweaters can distract or inhibit movement – remove these, tactfully, before the class begins.

6 A *quiet,* perceptive helper (adult) can tie shoe laces (double knots), wipe noses etc. so that the teacher is free to teach.

7 Observe natural movement of young children "in a free play" environment such as an outdoor playground. Children move differently from adults. It is not wise to impose adult mannerisms on young children. The teacher must observe and be interested in *child* movement.

8 The music and movement class is a "teacher-led" activity that requires careful planning if progress is to be made and interest maintained. There must be a curriculum plan and a logical lesson sequence.

9 Control of the group must be established at the beginning. As the children mature, they will gradually acquire self control. Falls and accidents cannot always be avoided, but the teacher should watch for potentially unsafe situations. Be ready to stop or redirect an unsafe activity *before* an accident happens.

10 It takes time and experience for a child to learn movement and listening skills. And it takes time, experience and ongoing study for a teacher to learn to direct music and movement activities. Movement is an important component of modern music education, especially with young beginners.

The reluctant child
The child who does not feel free to participate

This behaviour is familiar to the early childhood teacher – one child sits or stands, unhappily, on the sidelines. Though it may occur during any activity, it is particularly noticeable in movement games when all the other children are participating with joy. Experience will give the teacher the skill and patience required. Here are a few suggestions.

1 Wait until the child is ready to join the group. "Come and sit beside me, and watch for a while".

2 But do not wait too long. Many children, in the modern home, spend hours in front of a television set, passively watching someone else do things, and this has become a habit. Modern music education means active participation by every child and the teacher must find a way to charm or lead the reluctant child. Try to solve the problem in the first class before the child begins to think that active participation is for somebody else.

3 Try to understand how the child feels.

4 Is the activity or musical material *right* for the child? What interests the child? Try to incorporate it into the lesson.

5 Is the child feeling well? What happened before the class?

6 Be happy and encouraging if the child participates only for a minute e.g. tries a drum.

7 The teacher must build the child's trust. A light touch, a quiet sense of humour, and a warm interest in the child are essential. "I understand how you feel. I am on your side". The teacher's attitude could affect the child's feelings about music for life!

8 Invite the parent, or another adult, that the child knows and trusts, to join the class and act as a "helper" for the whole group. This may help the child to feel more secure and ready to participate.

This problem is a challenge to the teacher. As you get to know the children, you will find ways to encourage active participation by all the children to Move, Sing, Listen, and Play.

Equipment to encourage the child to move

This equipment adds interest and often stimulates or encourages the shy, inhibited child to "join in" movement games.

Have one piece of equipment for each child and usually, only one kind at a time.

Be aware of the child's physical development when choosing size, weight, length etc. Experiment yourself *before* the class time, to get the "feel" and the possibilities of the equipment.

Encourage children to explore and experiment with this equipment. Teach them to tidy (roll up or fold) and return to correct box when the activity is finished.

1 *Felt Ribbons* — Cut ribbons, three inches wide, from 72" (2 m) heavy, good quality coloured felt. ("Ribbon" will be 72" x 3").
   a) Hold one end of your ribbon. How can you make it move? high? low? quick? slow? all around you? Try holding it with the other hand and making it move.
   b) Hold both ends with both hands. How can you move your ribbon now?
   c) Make it into a hat — go for a walk; a belt; a scarf; a bandage for your sore arm. You don't need to tie it, because felt sticks to itself.
   d) Take your dog for a walk on a lead (pull ribbon along floor).
   e) Make it into a long line on your own floor space. Walk forwards on the "tight-rope"; walk backwards; what else?
   f) Make it into a circle in your space; jump in; jump out; jump in and out backwards; what else?
   g) The circle is a nest and you are a bird; sit in your nest; fly away from your nest — but be careful to fly *around* all the other nests; fly back to your nest; go to sleep in your nest.
Allow 10-20 seconds for each game. Ask the children for other ideas. No accompaniment needed.

2 Use instruments such as *jingles* or *maracas* when the child can move *and* play easily, at the same time.

3 Work out games with following equipment: *Scarf squares* — large 36" (1 m.) squares of assorted colours and designs. They can be made with light weight fabric. *Balls* — coloured tennis balls are attractive, the right size, and have a good covering for young children to hold. Try bounce, roll and "pass" games. *"Candles"* — balance a ball on the top of a 9" cardboard tube. Walk slowly, holding the "candle", pass from one hand to the other; place on the floor and "jump over the candlestick". Pick up the candle, without losing the ball etc. *Tile squares, rug squares* — samples with finished edges of assorted colours — to build shapes on the floor to simulate paths, buildings. . .

4 Equipment to stimulate interest, or clarify a concept. *Pictures and picture books.* Illustrations should be large and clear so that the whole class can see. If using a book, cover up extraneous material on the opposite page.
   Real flowers, leaves, sea shells etc.
   Dolls in costume; hand puppets.
   A music box for listening or dancing.

Further reading

Aronoff, F.: **Music and Young Children** (Expanded Edition) Turning Wheel Press, 1980
      Move with the Music Turning Wheel Press, 1982
Gell, H.: **Music, Movement and the Young Child** Australasian Publishing, Co., 1973
Gray and Percival: **Music, Movement and Mime** Oxford University Press, 1966
Haselbach, B.: **Improvisation, Dance, Movement** Magnamusic-Baton, 1976
Jaques-Dalcroze, E.: **Rhythm, Music and Education** (revised) Dalcroze Society, U.K., 1973
Vanderspaar, E.: **Dalcroze Handbook** 1985
Weikart, P.: **Movement Plus Music** High Scope Press, 1985
      Movement Plus Rhymes, Songs and Singing Games High Scope Press, 1988
Yelin, J.: **Movement That Fits** Summy-Birchard, 1990

Student project
a) Choose a game in this section. Write down the step by step teaching directions that you would *say* to a group of 4 year old children so that they could play the game happily *and* have the indicated musical experience.
b) Do it with a group and evaluate your work.

Learning to sing

All children can learn to sing.

If you can breathe, you can sing.

The more you sing, the better you sing.

The ability to sing is a firm foundation for any future music education. Children learn to sing by imitating a good model and by listening to a song that is repeated often. Children, who have heard singing from birth, learn to sing with ease. Singing begins with the babbling and chanting of infancy. Soon, the child begins to sing some of the words of a song with some idea of the melody. Then they follow along when the adult starts a song; and finally they should be able to start a song at the first word and sing it right through with accurate pitch, both in group singing or as a solo.

Help children who have not found their singing voices. Perhaps they have never sung before. Try some individual work, using small parts of a song, with echo technique. Change the pitch to where the child is singing, to show what "tone matching" sounds and feels like. Encourage the child by praising *any* improvement. Singing in a group gives support and helps children sing better. A singing game that repeats many times in the playing, is a natural way for children to develop their voices. Play the *starting note* on a xylophone, tone bar or piano. The teacher can start the song *without* an introduction or accompaniment; this trains the children to catch the pitch immediately. Or, the teacher can chant some "starting words", using the pitch of the *first note* of the song. A small action of pushing the rain away on the beat will encourage children to sing – see p. 92.

Introduction Start on A   Song

Let's all sing now Rain, rain go a - way, etc.

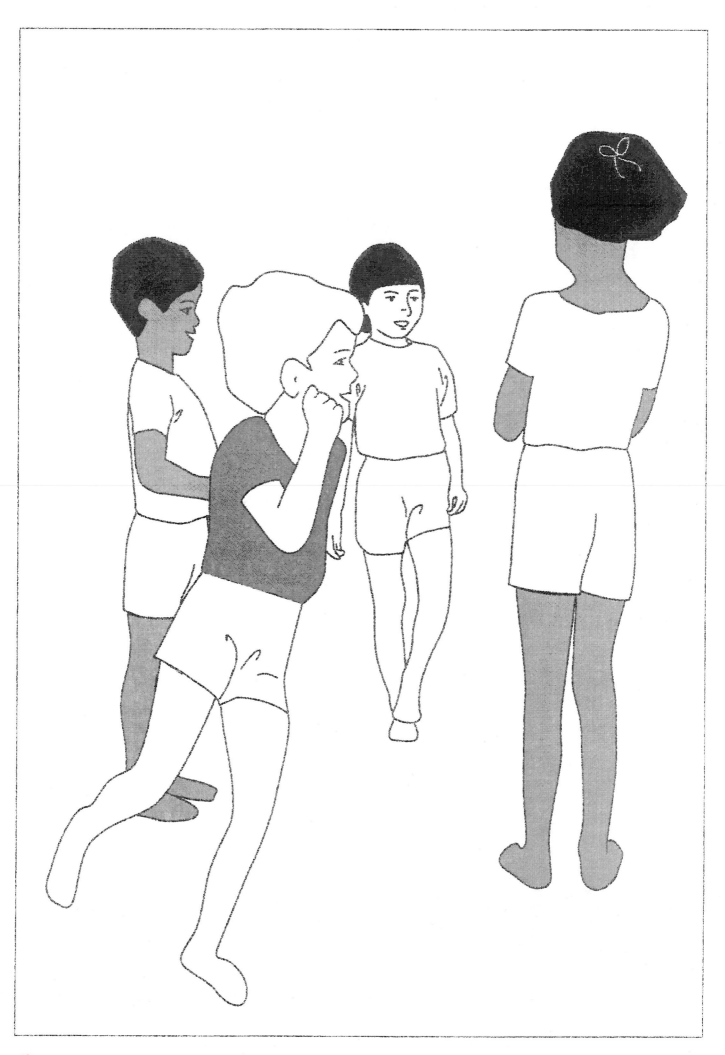

Musical experiences in the speech games, singing chants and singing games

Speech games

Introduction

"Language sings just as music speaks".
> Kati Forrai

"Babbling, in preparation for speech, begins as early as the second or third month of life".
> Helmut Moog

"It's the beat and the melody that count".
> Jay Ingram in *Talk, Talk, Talk*

The child who has enjoyed finger plays, nursery rhymes and speech games has received valuable musical experiences. In these games the child subconsciously hears and feels regular pulsation (beat), tempo, rhythm patterns, dynamics, pitch, tone colour and phrasing. These rhymes and finger plays can be done in a non-rhythmical way, but if musical learning is the goal, the parent or teacher will try to emphasize the musical elements as they say the rhymes. I have indicated the beat or pulse of rhymes with short vertical lines above the words that come "on the beat". Speech games prepare the child for Singing Chants and Singing Games.

Speech play games

These can be played by parent and child at the infant and toddler stage, but are enjoyed by older children, too. Keep a good eye contact with the child or children.

1 Walk Down the Path

Phrase feeling

Walk down the path – parent "walks" fingers up baby's face
Knock at the door –"knock" gently on forehead
Lift the latch –"lift" up nose
Wipe your feet – brush fingers across chin
And walk in – touch mouth

2 'Round About and 'Round About

Pitch change
Phrase feeling

'Round about and 'round about – Make circles on child's palm for first two lines
Runs a wee mouse
Up a bit, up a bit – walk fingers up child's arm (voice gets higher)
In a wee house – under child's arm

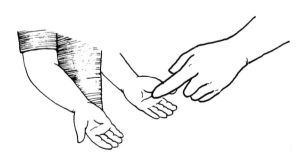

3 To Market, To Market

    | | | |
To market, to market, to buy a fat pig

    | | | |
Home again, home again, jiggety jig

    | | | |
To market, to market, to buy a fat hog

    | | | |
Home again, home again, jiggety jog.

A good knee bouncing or foot riding game. Older children can play the game with a doll or a favourite toy animal or teddy bear.

4 Humpty Dumpty Sat on a Wall

    | | | |
Humpty Dumpty sat on a wall
- Arms joined over head to make a big egg

    | | | |
Humpty Dumpty had a great fall
- Arms fall down to lap

    | | | |
All the King's horses and all the King's men
- Fingers march on lap (on the beat)

    | | | |
Couldn't put Humpty together again.
- Arms apart over head; (shake head sadly on the beat)

5 Little Miss Muffet

    | | | |
Little Miss Muffet sat on a tuffet
- Hands sitting on lap

    | | |
Eating her curds and whey.
- One hand is the dish, the other hand mimes eating from the dish.

    | | | |
Along came a spider who sat down beside her,
- Fingers of *one* hand crawl across lap and sit.

    | | |
And frightened Miss Muffet away.
- Other hand quickly goes behind back.

6 Little Jack Horner

| | | | |

Little Jack Horner sat in a corner,
- Sit in your place

    | | |

Eating his Christmas pie.
- Mime eating the pie

  | | | |

He put in his thumb and pulled out a plum,
- Put one thumb into pie, then show us the plum.

And said, "What a good boy am I".
- Clap hands quickly, following rhythm pattern *And said, "What a good boy am I".*

7 This Little Pig Went To Market

Phrase
Accent
Pitch
Tempo

This little pig went to market –	pull child's thumb or toe. Squeeze slightly on "this"
This little pig stayed home –	2nd finger
This little pig had roast beef –	3rd finger
This little pig had none –	4th finger
This little pig says "wee wee wee wee" –	5th finger, then walk your fingers up arm. Use a *higher* voice
all the way home	and a *faster* tempo.

Repeat with the other hand or foot. When the child is ready, parent and child could change roles.

Games for feeling the beat

"Catching" the beat and "keeping" the beat is a basic skill in music performance. We do not expect precision in the early years but these finger play games and rhymes teach the child, in a subconscious way, to "catch" and "keep" the beat. Use a natural comfortable tempo for the child.

Divided beat
1 Open them, shut them

A hand play game; open and close on the beat, as marked.

  | | | |

Open them, shut them, open them shut them

  | | |

Give them a little clap, yes!   nod head on "rest" beat.

  | | | |

Open them, shut them, open them, shut them

  | | |

Put them in your lap, yes!   nod head on "rest" beat.

2 Ride A Cock Horse

This rhyme is in $\frac{6}{8}$ meter. Be sure the "horse" moves on the beat – 2 to a bar

| | | | |

Ride a cock horse to Banbury Cross

| | | |

To see a fine lady upon a white horse

| | | |

With rings on her fingers and bells on her toes

| | | |

She shall have music where ever she goes.

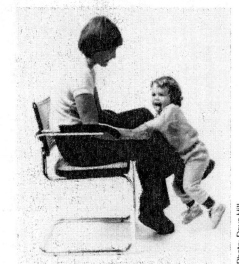

Photo: Dave Hill

3 Andy Pandy Sugary Candy

| | | | | | |

*Andy Pandy Sugary Candy, All Pop **Down***

| | | | | | |

*Andy Pandy Sugary Candy, All Pop **Up***

| | | | | | |

*Andy Pandy Sugary Candy, All Pop **In***

| | | | | | |

*Andy Pandy Sugary Candy, All Pop **Out**.*

Standing *Circle* formation: Clap 4 Beats and follow words –
Pop Down, Up, Into circle, then out.

4 Hickory Dickory Dock

| | | ♩

Hickory Dickory Dock

• Stand tall to be a grandfather clock. Hang arms to be the pendulum which swings on the beat.

| | | ♩

The mouse ran up the clock.

• Fingers are the mice, running up from feet to head.

| |

The Clock struck "One"

• Clap hands loudly over head on *"One"*

| |

The Mouse ran down.

• Mice fingers run down body from head to feet.

| | | ♩

Hickory Dickory Dock.

• Arms become pendulum swinging back and forth on the beat.

5 The Grand Old Duke of York

This rhyme has a marching tempo. It is usually sung, but it is also effective as a *spoken* rhyme. The children march and swing their arms, like a Duke, for the first part; they clap and use high, low and normal speech pitch in the 2nd part. Set pace with some "starting" words (Introduction).

| | | | |
Left, Right, Left, Right

The Grand old Duke of York (Right)   – step beat

He had ten thousand men (Right)   – step beat

He marched them up to the top of the hill   – step beat

Pitch

And marched them down again (Halt).   – step beat

High voice   *O when you're up you're up* (Yes), – clap hands high above head

Low voice   *And when you're down you're down (Yes),* – clap hands down near hips

Normal voice   *And when you're only half way up* – clap hands near head

You're neither up nor down. (Halt). – continue to clap hands near head

(Repeat 1st 4 lines, and end on Halt)

The words in brackets at the end of the lines (Right, Halt and Yes) give the correct time space for the "rest".

Games for feeling tempo – faster and slower

Give the children experiences where they can keep a natural, comfortable beat, before introducing "faster" or "slower".

1 The Slow Train

Slower   *Choo! Choo! Choo! Choo!, The train goes up the track now*

Choo! Choo! Choo! Choo!, the train goes down the track now
slide palms of hands together, slowly

The Fast Train

Faster

| | | | | | | |

Choo choo choo choo The train goes up the track now

Choo Choo Choo Choo The train goes down the track now

– slide palms together, quickly. Don't let it run away – keep it steady. Use a moderate voice for both "slowly" and "quickly". When the children are ready to think of two things at once, see if they can speak slowly *and* loudly or quickly *and* softly.

2 Eeny, meeny

Eeny meeny miny moe, catch a tiger by the toe.

If he hollers let him go, eeny, meeny, miny, moe.

Which tempo?

Speak with *moderate tempo*, patting legs on the beat (patchen).
Ask children for the name of another animal that goes very slowly.
Repeat rhyme to *slow beat*, putting in the slow animal's name (turtle)
Ask for the name of an animal that goes very quickly.
Repeat rhyme to *quick beat*, putting in the quick animal's name (fox)
Continue with other animals, after deciding whether it goes *fast* or *slow*.

Counting out rhymes

This is a natural way for children to select who is to be "it" for a game. It is also a fine game to give the children the feeling of the on-going beat.

On-going beat

1 "Eeny meeny" is the traditional game for this.

The teacher or a child goes around circle, "touching fists" until the last word. Use a slow tempo, at first. The child, whose fist is touched on the word "moe", is "it".

Beat

2 A shorter rhyme for finding "it"

Sky Blue

| | | | | | | |
Sky blue, sky blue, who's it? It's you.
Note: the traditional rhyme that older children use says *"not you"*, which is *not* appropriate for young children.

Speech games for feeling rhythm patterns

Rhythm

a) Give the children some experience feeling and showing a steady beat before introducing rhythm patterns.
b) Use words and short sequences that interest children.
c) Use a physical motion with the words i.e. tap, clap, pat.
d) Use a moderate voice and tempo at first. When the children are ready, change tempo, dynamics or tone colour.
e) Speak clearly, slightly emphasizing the rhythmic element, but keep the natural rhythm of the language, as spoken.
f) Give the feeling of a phrase length i.e. repeat a name or word four times.

Rhythm In A Rhyme

Roses Are Red (4-6)

Roses are Red, Violets are Blue

Honey is sweet and so are you.

Follow the rhythm of the words with clapping hands. Try it on rhythm sticks or a hand drum. Then try to play the rhythm while you say the words silently (*inside*) for development of *inner hearing*.

1 Names and words:

The teacher's name
clap

say: Mrs. Wood, Mrs. Wood, Mrs. Wood, Mrs. Wood
or: Don-na Wood

Note: I do not use *children's* names this way. It may be uncomfortable for them.

Try the name of your school; a street; a city; a country; animal names etc.

Animal name games

Rhythm

Clap ♩ ♩ ♩ ♩
&
Say *chip-munk chip-munk*

Chipmunk

Clap ♫ ♫ ♫ ♫
&
Say *bun-ny rab-bit bun-ny rab-bit*

Bunny rabbit

Clap ♫ ♩ ♫ ♩
&
Say *Pol-ar bear Pol-ar bear*

Polar bear

Clap ♩   ♩
&
Say *Moose Moose*
(to give the feeling of "two beats", clap on beat one and make a silent downward motion on beat two).

Moose

Clap ♩ ♫ ♩ ♫
&
Say *wood-pecker wood-pecker*

Woodpecker

Name games with pictures

Trace and mount each picture on a large card, so all can see.
Set up on the wall or a table, at the *eye level of the children.*

Clap ♩ ♩ ♩ ♩ ♩ ♩ ♩ ♩
&
Say *chip-munk chip-munk chip-munk chip-munk*

Clap ♫ ♫ ♫ ♫ ♫ ♫ ♫ ♫
&
Say *bun-ny rab-bit bun-ny rab-bit bun-ny rab-bit bun-ny rab-bit*

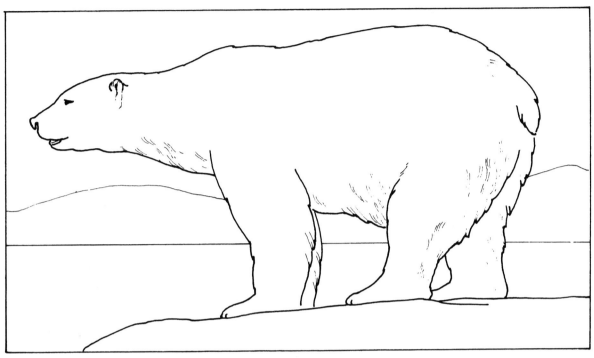

Clap &

Say *Pol-ar bear Pol-ar bear Pol-ar bear Pol-ar bear*

Clap &

Say *Moose Moose Moose Moose*

Clap   ♩ ♫ ♩ ♫ ♩ ♫ ♩ ♫
&

Say *wood-pecker wood-pecker wood-pecker wood-pecker*

Learning to read and write rhythm patterns (6-8)

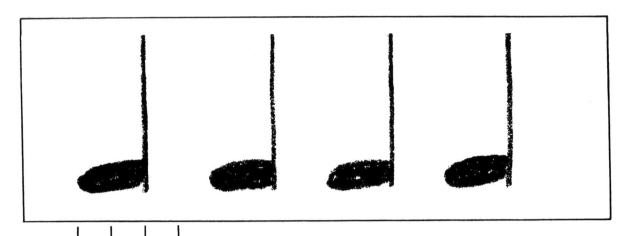

- Clap
- Say   chip-munk chip-munk
- Write on blackboard or paper

- Clap
- Say   Bun-ny rab-bit, bun-ny rab-bit
- Write on blackboard or paper

2 Word sequences

Clap and say these rhythm patterns

a
Chip-munk Bun-ny rab-bit

b
Po-lar Bear Moose

c
Wood-pec-ker Chip-munk Bun-ny rab-bit Moose

Change the word sequence and make a different rhythm pattern.

Use simple combinations of ♩, ♫ and 𝅗𝅥 for young children.

Play them on simple percussion instruments such as rhythm sticks or drums.

When the children are ready, introduce rhythm symbols. First they recognize and read the symbols ♩, ♫, 𝅗𝅥 and then they can write them on the blackboard or on plain paper. (Staff lines are not needed until they notate pitch and melody).Children can also clap and say duration syllables (see p. 184).

See if they can "think" the words *"inside"* and clap or tap the rhythm on the "outside" (inner hearing).

3 Children's Fête or Holiday words

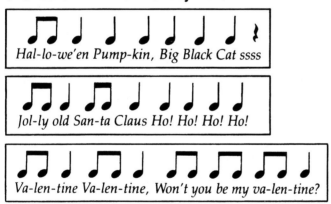

Ask the children for other word suggestions for these rhythm games.

4 Playground sayings

Children's lore, and short sayings, offer good material for rhythm pattern sequences.

— clap, pat, tap, step or play on percussion instruments.
— keep the words "inside" and clap the *rhythm* pattern.
— pat the *beat* on your legs while you say the words.

– The children keep the *beat*; the teacher claps the *rhythm*.
– Do the opposite. Let the children clap the rhythm several times *before* the teacher comes in. This prepares the children for "canon", and simple ostinati when they are a little older.
– Clap and say rhythm patterns with duration syllables (ta, ti ti, ta-a).
– Spread these activities over several lessons. Young children tire easily, and then the clapping becomes monotonous and unmusical. Shake wrists between clapping games.

Feeling the rest

The rest is a measured silence. It is a natural place to take a breath, in rhymes and songs. It is an important element in rhythm and needs to be presented with care.

The rest can be felt by saying a word – see "The Grand Old Duke of York (Right; Halt; Yes) page 74.

The rest can be felt by making a sound – see "Big Black Cat (sss) page 82.

The rest can be felt with a small motion with the hands as in the following rhyme:

Peas Porridge Hot
Hold 2 rounded hands together to make the porridge pot
Shake a little on the beat and "open the lid" on the rest

| | | | | | | | |
Peas por-ridge hot, (Rest) *peas por-ridge cold* (Rest)

Peas por-ridge in a pot, nine days old (Rest)

Peas por-ridge hot   ("open the lid" and blow on 𝄽 [rest])

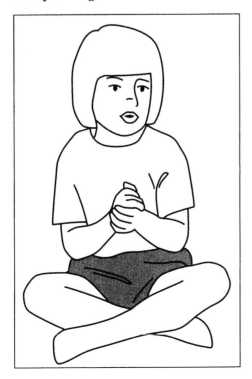

Copycat or echo games

The children learn to *listen* first and then, to imitate a rhythm pattern. With young children, it is better and more meaningful to clap rhythm patterns *with spoken words*.
"Listen when I do it; *then* you copy me".

First the teacher | Then the children echo

It is better to have a rest, or breathing space at the end of each line in first echo experiences. The teacher can then point to the children when it is time to echo.

Teacher | Children

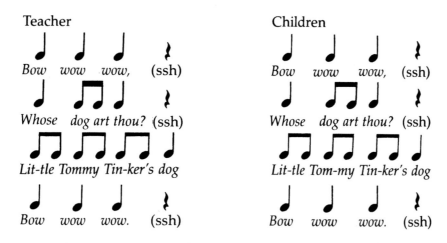

The (ssh) indicates the rest space.

Choose a rhyme that has a *different* rhythm pattern in each line
e.g., Clap, Clap, Clap 93; Bow wow wow 84; A.B.C. 85

A. B. C.

Listen carefully to the 3rd and 4th line of this rhyme. The eighth notes ♪ and rests ↗ require a quick reaction. The third line begins with a "pick-up sound" or anacrusis.

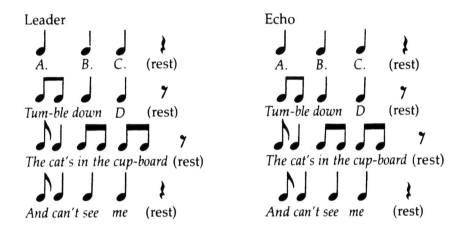

Leader

A.　B.　C.　(rest)

Tum-ble down　D　(rest)

The cat's in the cup-board (rest)

And can't see　me　(rest)

Echo

A.　B.　C.　(rest)

Tum-ble down　D　(rest)

The cat's in the cup-board (rest)

And can't see　me　(rest)

When children have had echo game experience, try "Question and Answer" games.

Question and answer games

Start with rhymes that have the "question and answer" idea in the text.
In the "copycat" or echo game, the 2nd phrase is the *same* as the first phrase.
In the question and answer game, the 2nd phrase is *different*.

1 Pussycat – Say the words to bring out their meaning.

Question	*Answer*
Pussycat, Pussycat, where have you been?	*I've been to London to visit the Queen.*
Pussycat, Pussycat, what did you there?	*I frightened a little mouse under the chair.*

1. Teacher asks question; group answers.
2. Group asks question; one child answers.
3. One child asks question; another child answers.

2 Birthday Game Rhyme
The group asks the question, patting knees on the beat or the rhythm pattern

|　|　|　|　|

Ap-ples, pea-ches, pears and plums,

|　|　|　|　|

Tell us when your birth-day comes.

First child answers and *claps* the *rhythm pattern* of birthday Ja-nu-a-ry six-teenth
Group repeats: Ap-ples, pea-ches etc.

Second child answers and claps the rhythm pattern:

May 4th;

or: I don't know

or: Next week

Continue with group asking the question and each child in turn giving an answer while clapping the rhythm pattern of the words. Birthdays are a favorite subject, but some may not know the actual day, so be ready to help.

3 Who made the pie?

Group question

Child in middle of circle answers

Who made the pie? — *I did*

Who stole the pie? — *He/she did* (points to a child)

Who found the pie? — *He/she did* (points to another child)

Who ate the pie? — *We all did* (all answer)

4 Whither goest thou?

Group in a circle, ask questions to "it" in the middle

Q. *Lit-tle girl, lit-tle girl whi-ther go-est thou?*
     boy,   boy

A. *Down in the mea-dow   to feed my cow*

"Could you think of another place to go? What would you do there?"
This is the beginnings of improvisation. It doesn't need to rhyme and don't try to get equal phrase lengths in "question and answer", yet.

5 What did you see on your way to school?

Teacher or a child asks the same short question to each child in a group. Each child should give a different answer. Use speech alone, at first, then say the words *and* clap the rhythm pattern. To give the answer more rhythmic interest, encourage short sentence answers, rather than just one word.

Q. What did you see on the way to school?

A. I saw a dog

or A. A great big gar-bage truck

or A. My friend Bil-ly

6 Hello, Hello, Hello, Sir

Question	Answer
Hello, Hello, Hello Sir. Won't you come out and play, Sir?	*No. Sir.*
Why Sir?	*Because I've got a cold, Sir.*
Where did you get your cold, Sir?	*At the North Pole, Sir.*
What were you doing there, Sir?	*Catching polar bears, Sir.*
How many did you catch, Sir?	*One Sir, Two Sir, Three Sir and that's enough for me, Sir.*

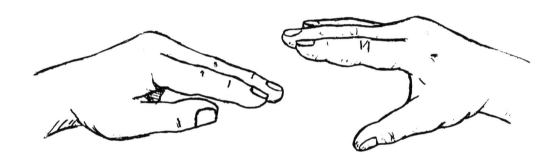

The spoken word is *important* to children. Early rhythm games should include *speech*. Later, "inner hearing" can be developed by "thinking" the words "inside" while clapping, tapping or playing an instrument in the rhythm pattern.

Books of nursery rhymes, finger plays and children's lore

Alison, C.: **I'll Tell You A Story, I'll Sing You A Song** Delacourte Press, New York, 1988
Baring-Gould: **The Annotated Mother Goose** World Publishing, 1967
Fowke, E.: **Sally Go Round the Sun** McClelland and Stewart, 1969
Forrai, K. and Sinor, J.: **Music in Preschool** Corvina, 1994 (2nd ed.)
Lines, K.: **Lavender's Blue** Oxford University Press, 1965
Matterson, E.: **This Little Puffin** Penguin Books, 1972
Opie, I. and P.: **The Puffin Book of Nursery Rhymes** Penguin Books, 1971
Taylor, D. and J.: **Learning With Traditional Rhymes** Lady Bird Books, 1976

... **Finger Rhymes**	... **Number Rhymes**	... **Memory Rhymes**
... **Talking Rhymes**	... **Action Rhymes**	... **Dancing Rhymes**
... **Singing Rhymes**	... **Skipping Rhymes**	

Student project

Make a collection of words, sayings and rhymes in which the children can experience the elements of music. Show the beat first and then later the rhythm pattern of the words.

Singing chants

Chanting and improvising with words and snatches of melody develop from the musical babbling of infancy. Parents who sing and play "baby games" with their children encourage musical responses, and these children usually learn to sing with ease and joy. Children who have not been stimulated musically by "live" music (e.g. music from a real person, close to the child, as opposed to recordings, T.V., radio or "stage" entertainers) may have not "found" their singing voices. They may not know the difference between making a speaking "sound" and a singing "sound".

Finding the child's singing voice

I play this game with a 3-5 year old group when I hear uncertain, monotone or speaking sounds. (Be very tactful with non-singers – ignore the situation for a while.)

1 Where is your voice?
   a) Where does your singing voice come from? your mouth? your throat?
   b) Hold your hand over your throat. Can you feel your voice when you speak?
   c) Does your singing voice **feel** different from your speaking voice?

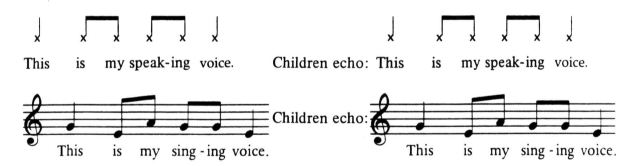

"One to one" chanting and singing helps uncertain singers, provided this child is given *time* to learn, without feeling that there is a big problem. The child will *feel* and *hear* what "tone matching" is, if the parent or teacher takes up the *same pitch* as the child. The repetition of group singing games is helpful for uncertain singers. Encourage these children and be ready to praise their efforts when there is the smallest progress.

Current research tells us that the young child's comfortable and musical singing voice range lies from middle C or D and up to G or A, a range of 5-6 notes/tones. Many teachers want to sing in a lower pitch than C-A with the children, often causing "off-key" singing or yelling. On the other hand, standard collections of children's songs in the past were often set too high, which also fosters off-key singing or *no* singing. Choose songs that are set in the most comfortable pitch and range for *the young child*.

Tone matching games

1 **A musical beginning for a class.** The teacher can make a note about each child's singing development.

Teacher

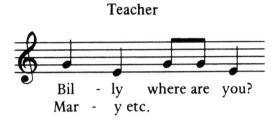

Bil - ly where are you?
Mar - y etc.

Child

Here I am.

George ___ where are you? (absent)

All children

He's not here.

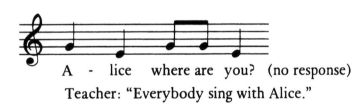

A - lice where are you? (no response)
Teacher: "Everybody sing with Alice."

All children

Here I am.

An - na where are you?

Here I am.
(low speak-sing)
Teacher: "Anna has a lower voice."

An - na where are you?

Here I am.
(approximately)

2 Singing the roll call
Change the melody pattern for each name
Keep a record of each child's "pitch" development

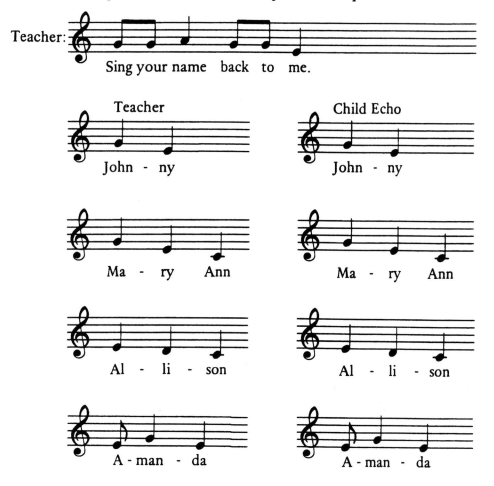

Teacher: Sing your name back to me.

Teacher — John - ny

Child Echo — John - ny

Ma - ry Ann

Ma - ry Ann

Al - li - son

Al - li - son

A - man - da

A - man - da

If you make a tape recording of this game several times during the year, you will be able to assess the voice and listening development of each child. Children enjoy hearing their voices "on tape". Sometimes a "non-singer" will suddenly discover how to sing!

Chanting words. Improvising. Playground chants.

Picture books with large clear pictures of animals, birds, flowers or toys stimulate singing improvisations. Start with single words, repeating each four times.

Mon-key   Dan-de-li-on   Red-head-ed wood-pec-ker

Encourage the children to improvise chants into longer phrases
"The mon-key likes to swing"
"Dan-de-li-ons are yel-low"
"The red head-ed woodpecker lives in a tree"

Singing conversations, nonsense words and animal or bird sounds, using the singing voice strengthen vocal cords, develop the ear and encourage improvisation. Parents report that there is a noticeable increase in improvisational singing at home when children have "found" their voices through chants.
Ego building playground chants

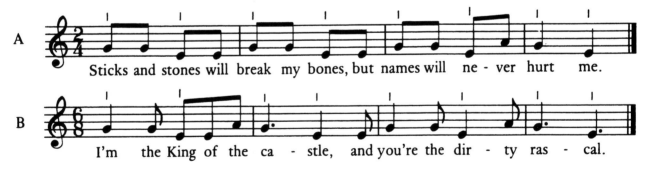

A   Sticks and stones will break my bones, but names will ne - ver hurt me.

B   I'm the King of the ca - stle, and you're the dir - ty ras - cal.

Sing these in an A.B.A. form. Include a repetitive clap, tap or patting action on the beat. This arrangement is a simple example of mixed meter $\frac{2}{4} - \frac{6}{8}$

When I was a child, we used these playground chants to boost self-esteem. Subconsciously, we were learning to sing in a natural child-like way with a falling minor 3rd.

Books with Singing Chants
Aronoff, F.: **Music and Young Children** Turning Wheel Press, New York, 1980
Forrai, K. (trans. Sinor, Jean): **Music in Preschool** Corvina, 1994

Songs and games with the children's chant

This is an important stage in learning to sing with joy and confidence. If we are to start "where the child is", in terms of singing and hearing abilities, we must select songs with a small range that follow the rhythms of the language of children. Do not omit or rush through this stage. The chants beginning on this page help children find their singing voices.

Good nursery schools and day care centres choose equipment such as toys, books, furniture, playground apparatus with great care. In this, they consider the stages of child development, the abilities and skills of children, learning goals and the formation of good taste. A learning toy of music is the *song* and it should be selected with as much care as a nursery school toy. At least once in each music period, there should be a song which helps the child to learn to sing in pitch and with good diction. All the songs in this section are in this category.

Relative pitch names are written above each song (s,m,l). It is an easy way for the teacher to learn to read music, but it has little meaning for children until the age of 6 or 7 (see page 188).

Traditional game-songs have been used by many generations of children to teach themselves to sing. *All voices can be developed.* When the children sing well in a group, ask several of them "can you sing by yourself?" In time, all the children should be able to sing by themselves.

Rain, rain, go away
(2-5) l s m

Finger play: Push the rain away with both hands, on the beat.
Improvise: Change "rain" to wind, snow, sun or fog.

See saw
(3-5) l s m

Activity: Sit on the floor with arms outstretched. Rock sideways on the beat.

Clap clap clap your hands
(2-4) l s m

Clap,   clap,   clap your hands,   Clap your hands to - ge - ther.
Pat,   pat,   pat your knees,   Pat your knees to - ge - ther.
Blink,   blink,   blink your eyes,   Blink your eyes to - ge - ther.

Improvisation: Ask the children for actions where they can feel the beat.

Standing: Swing, Swing, Swing your arms . . . sway with me . . . jump with me, etc.
Moving: Walk, Walk, Walk with me . . . walking all together . . .
Playing: Play, Play, Play your drum . . . your bells . . .

Starlight
(3-5) l s m

Star - light,   star   bright,   first   star   I've   seen   to - night,

Wish   I   may,   wish   I   might,   have   the   wish   I   wish   to - night.

Finger play: Point up to a different star on each beat
Improvise: Ask each child to wish for something. Then ask each child to tell the class about it with
a *singing voice.* "I wish for a bounc-ing ball; a new doll; an ice cream cone; a ba-by sis-ter . . . . .

Bye baby bunting
(2-5) s m l

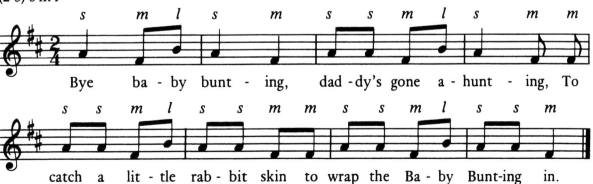

Bye   ba - by   bunt - ing,   dad -dy's gone   a - hunt - ing, To

catch   a   lit - tle   rab - bit   skin   to wrap   the   Ba - by   Bunt-ing   in.

Action: Hold a real doll or a "pretend" baby. Rock and sing to your baby.

Jack be nimble
(3-5) l s m

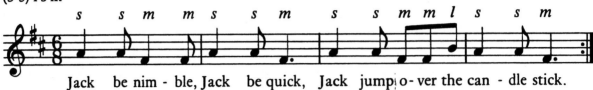

Jack   be nim - ble, Jack   be quick,   Jack   jump o - ver the can - dle stick.

Formation: Stationary circle, sitting or standing.
Equipment: A candle holder or a block placed in middle of the circle.
Game: Each child in turn, on the word "jump", goes over the "candle stick" and then jumps back over when the song is repeated. Substitute the child's real name for "Jack" i.e. Betty be nimble; then Johnny be nimble . . . .

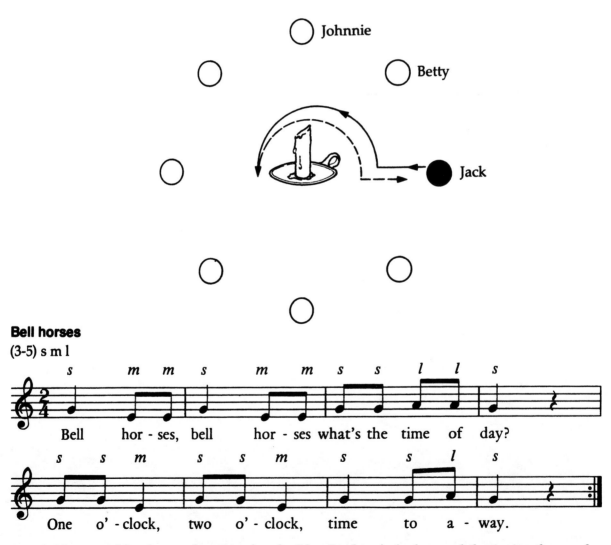

Bell horses
(3-5) s m l

Bell   hor - ses, bell   hor - ses what's the   time   of   day?

One   o' - clock,   two   o' - clock,   time   to   a - way.

The children stand in place and pat one hand with a jingle, on the beat, while singing the words. Repeat the song with the teacher singing while the children gallop away around the room.

Engine, Engine Number nine

(4-5) s m l
Speech introduction:
Choo! Choo! Choo! Choo!

Divided beat

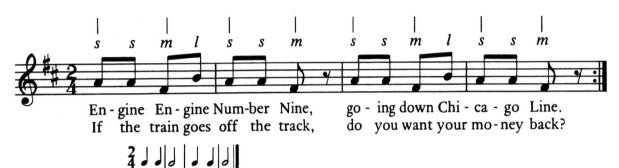

Speech interlude: Yes I do, Yes I do!

Repeat song — "Engine Engine"

Formation: Each child sits "in an engine" in a good space, with knees bent slightly and elbows bent slightly.

Game: Speech introduction: Move arms back and forth on Choo! Choo!

Song: Push legs and arms back and forth on the beat (2 to a bar)

Interlude: Clap rhythm pattern

Song: as before

When the children feel the beat with rhythmic sureness, repeat the game from a standing position. They need to lift their knees up, to catch the *quarter note beat,* when the melody rhythm moves in *eighth notes.* The trains can stay on their own track and go where they please (without bumping), or they can move in several lines. Change the leader often.

Lucy locket (3-4)

Here is a song with a 4-note range for children who have not learned to sing.

l s m

Phrase feeling

Lu - cy Loc - ket lost her poc - ket, Kit - ty Fi - sher found it.

Not a pen - ny was there in it, On - ly rib - bon 'round it.

Formation: stationary circle, standing.

Equipment: a flat purse (not too small) tied with ribbon.

Game: Use a counting out rhyme p. 75, to choose "Lucy".

Phrase 1) Lucy, with her purse, walks inside circle and drops it on the floor in front of Kitty.

Phrase 2) Kitty picks up the purse and catches up to Lucy.

Phrase 3) and 4) Lucy and Kitty hold the purse between them and walk around inside circle. At end of verse, Lucy *sits* in her place. The game continues, with Kitty becoming Lucy, until all the children have had a turn. The children must be ready to fit the actions to the music. For the chase version (5-6), see *Music in Preschool* by Forrai, K. and Sinor, Corvina.

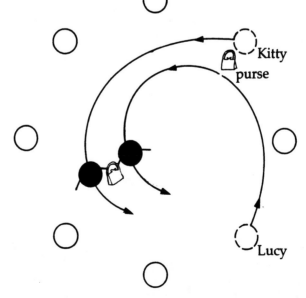

* The melody sequence from s to l is sometimes difficult. Singing with "hand levels" may help

               Locket

Lucy   lost her

                       pocket

Charlie over the ocean

(4-5) s m

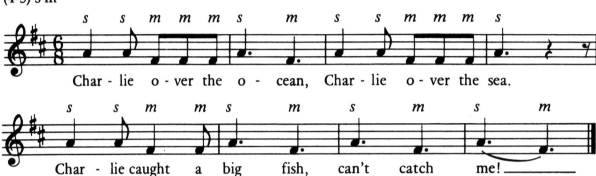

Char - lie o - ver the o - cean, Char - lie o - ver the sea.

Char - lie caught a big fish, can't catch me!

Formation: a large stationary circle (the ocean), standing.

Choose Charlie with a counting out game (page 75).

Game: Charlie walks around the *outside* of the circle. On the word "caught", Charlie touches the nearest child on the back. "Charlie" runs around the circle with "caught" child chasing him. "Charlie" sits in space left by "caught".

"Caught" becomes the new Charlie as the game repeats until all have had a turn. With each "Charlie" *sitting* down at the end of each verse, it will be obvious to all the children, who has not had a turn.

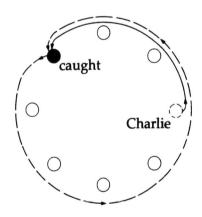

Picture Books based on songs (music included)

Aliki: **Hush Little Baby** Prentice Hall

Langstaff, J.: **On Christmas Day In The Morning** Harcourt Brace & Company

Over In The Meadow Harcourt Brace and Company

Spier, P.: **The Fox Went Out On A Chilly Night** Doubleday

To Market, To Market Doubleday

London Bridge Is Falling Down Doubleday

Student project

Make a short study of a child who does not sing with the group. Observe this child over several weeks and note any progress. Suggest 5 techniques that you could try to encourage the child to sing with the class.

Singing games

The songs in this section follow the three note chants of the last section, in a developmental order. After finding the singing voice and gaining a sense of pitch, the vocal range is gradually extended in these (voice teaching) development songs. At least one song of this type should be included in each class lesson to develop singing skills. The teacher can, and indeed should, sing diatonic songs of wider range with more complicated rhythms *to* the children. Wider range songs can accompany and direct the action in movement games (see page 59, Roll My Ball) and also can be used for listening experiences when the teacher sings and the children listen and move.

Sing all songs naturally with clear diction and good pitch. A teacher who knows the joy of singing will pass on this joy to the children.

Teddy bear, Teddy bear
(3-4-5) s m r d

Formation: Circle *or* random spaces, standing
Game: Do appropriate action on the words:
"turn around" – take 3 steps
"touch the ground" – touch 3 times
"shine your shoe" – rub 3 times
"that will do" – clap 3 times

I see the moon
(4-5) s m d

Melody — Denise Bacon

Formation: Circle or random spaces
Game: Your hand is the moon — put it up in the sky.
Use hand levels to show where the moon goes *and where your voice goes.*

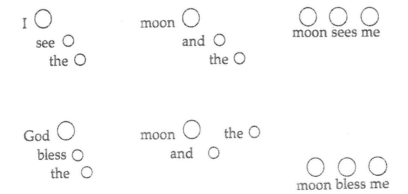

This prepares the child for future sight singing, ear training, and music writing.

Mary had a little lamb

(3-4-5) s m r d

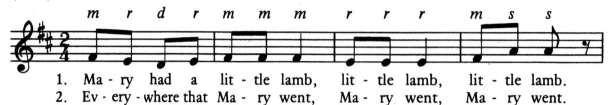

1. Ma - ry had a lit - tle lamb, lit - tle lamb, lit - tle lamb.
2. Ev - ery - where that Ma - ry went, Ma - ry went, Ma - ry went.

Ma - ry had a lit - tle lamb with fleece as white as snow.
Ev - ery - where that Ma - ry went the lamb was sure to go.

Formation: A large standing circle with a space between each child.

Game: Choose "Mary" with a counting out game.

Verse   1) Mary *walks* inside circle. At the end of the verse, she chooses the lamb.

2) Mary *runs* in and out between the children standing in the circle. The lamb runs behind Mary and "goes wherever she goes".

3) At the end of the verse, Mary goes back to her place and sits down. The lamb becomes Mary and the game continues from the beginning.

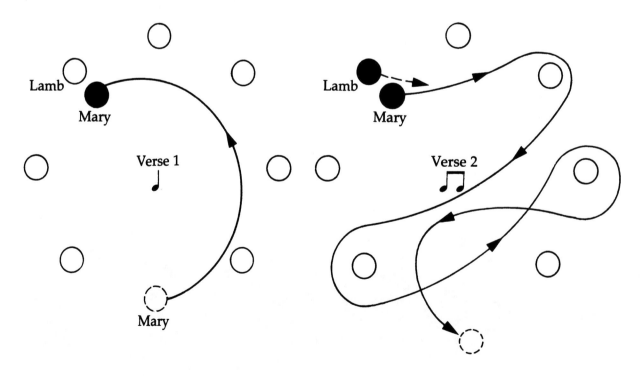

Ring around a rosy

(4-5) l s m d

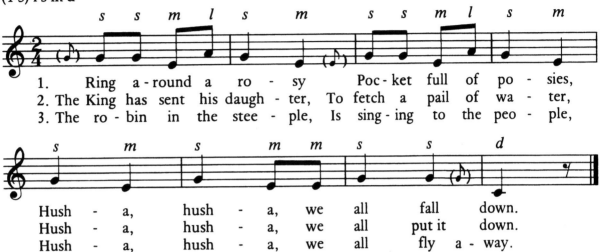

s	s	m	l	s	m	s	s	m	l	s	m

1. Ring a - round a ro - sy Poc - ket full of po - sies,
2. The King has sent his daugh - ter, To fetch a pail of wa - ter,
3. The ro - bin in the stee - ple, Is sing - ing to the peo - ple,

s	m	s	m	m	s	s	d

Hush - a, hush - a, we all fall down.
Hush - a, hush - a, we all put it down.
Hush - a, hush - a, we all fly a - way.

Formation: Choose a partner; stand in a good space and face each other, holding hands.

Game: Verse 1) partners make a small circle, turning bodies slightly in direction they are going. At the end, fall down softly — that's what "Hush-a" means!

Slower tempo Verse 2) partners pretend to carry a heavy pail of water between them as they walk and sing, *slowly*. Put the pail down carefully at the end of the verse.

Verse 3) partners face each other, holding hands up high to make a steeple. At the end, the children become birds and fly around the room. The teacher could improvise 8 bars of words and melody about "flying home" to make a suitable ending for this game.

Transposition The teacher can raise the pitch one or two tones (start on A or B) to bring out the steeple idea in verse 3.

Hop old squirrel

(3-4) m r d

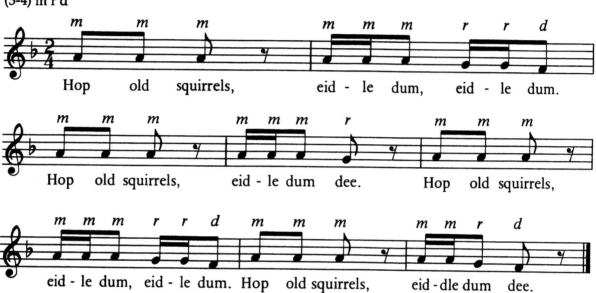

Hop old squirrels, eid - le dum, eid - le dum.

Hop old squirrels, eid - le dum dee. Hop old squirrels,

eid - le dum, eid - le dum. Hop old squirrels, eid - dle dum dee.

Finger play: Children sitting, formation optional.

The child's hands are "squirrels" that hop around on the child's lap — on the beat.

or

Game formation: standing stationary circle

Two or three children (squirrels) hop around "on all fours", inside the circle. The other children sing and clap on the beat. Let all the children have a turn, if possible.

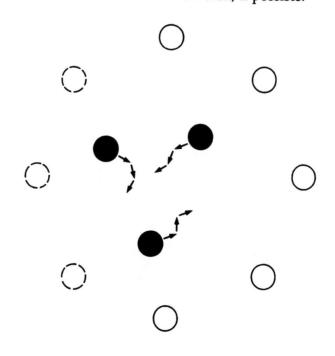

I've lost the closet key

(4-5-6) m r d

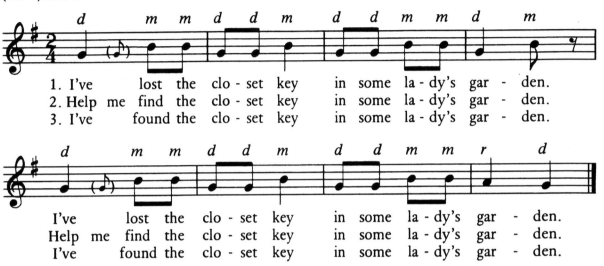

1. I've	lost the clo - set key	in some la - dy's gar -	den.
2. Help me find the clo - set key		in some la - dy's gar -	den.
3. I've	found the clo - set key	in some la - dy's gar -	den.

I've lost the clo - set key in some la - dy's gar - den.

Help me find the clo - set key in some la - dy's gar - den.

I've found the clo - set key in some la - dy's gar - den.

Formation: stationary standing circle; all children hold their hands behind their backs. Choose "it".

Equipment: a large door key.

Game: Verse 1) "it" walks, holding key, around *outside* of circle. "It" puts key into a child's hands.

Verse 2) "It" *turns,* and walks around *outside* of circle in the *opposite* direction. The child, standing in the circle, with the key must keep it "secretly" throughout this verse.

Verse 3) The child with the key holds it up for all to see while *walking inside* the circle. "It" and all the children stand and clap on the beat.

The child with the key goes outside the circle with the key and continues the game. The original key holder goes back to circle place, putting hands in front — so all will know who has had a turn.

Here comes a bluebird

(4-5) l s m r d

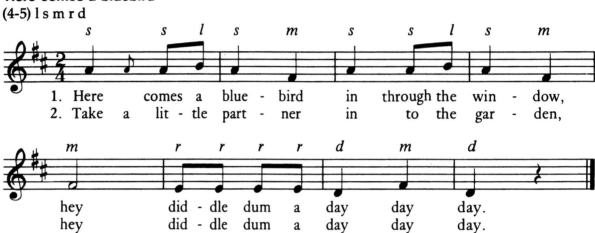

1. Here comes a blue - bird in through the win - dow,
2. Take a lit - tle part - ner in to the gar - den,

hey did - dle dum a day day day.
hey did - dle dum a day day day.

Formation: large standing circle, with spaces for "windows".

Choose the bluebird with a "counting out" game.

Game: Verse 1) The bluebird flies through the windows, in and out.

Verse 2) The bluebird chooses a partner and takes him or her into the middle of the circle *before bar 4.* The two children face each other and each claps the rhythm pattern of the last 4 bars.

Hey! diddle dum-a day day day

The first bluebird goes back to space in circle and sits down, showing that he or she had a turn.

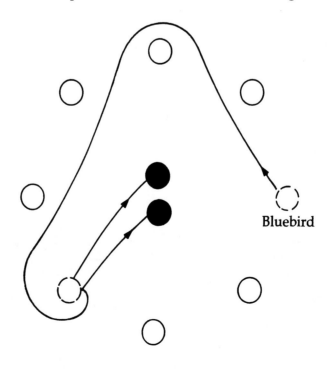

Bluebird

Here sits a monkey

(3-4-5) l s f m r d

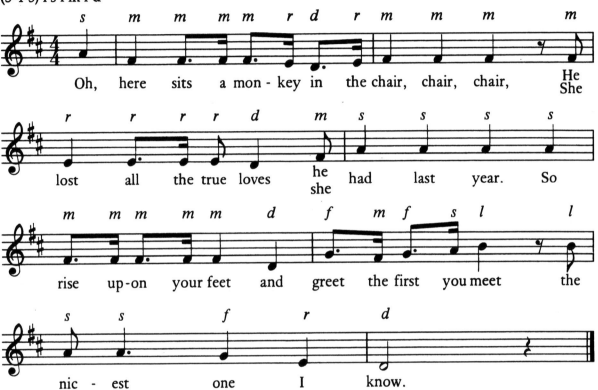

Formation: sitting or standing circle

Equipment: a low chair or a stool in the middle of the circle

Game: Choose the monkey with a "counting out" rhyme.

Line 1 and 2 The monkey sits on the chair. The children clap and sing.

Line 3 The monkey "rises" and "chooses" the next child to be the animal on the chair. The new child tells us which animal to sing about (fox, dragon, elephant, etc.). Each child is a different animal, on the chair.

Fuzzy wuzzy

(5-6) s m d

Melody-Denise Bacon

Circus bear dance

Formation: standing circle. Children stand on their "back feet" like circus bears with "front paws" extending forwards. *Try* several *slow* bear steps (♩ ♩ ♩ ♩) in this position rocking slightly from side to side.

Dance: Phrase 1) bears walk 4 slow steps *forwards* '(♩ ♩ ♩ ♩)
         Phrase 2) bears walk 4 slow steps *backwards* (♩ ♩ ♩ ♩)
         Phrase 3) bears clap hands (paws) 4 times, slowly (♩ ♩ ♩ ♩)
         Ending 4) 2 quick steps ♫ on "was he".

In this dance the children experience the feeling of stepping in ♩ while they sing ♫

The old gray cat

(4-5) mdt, l, s,

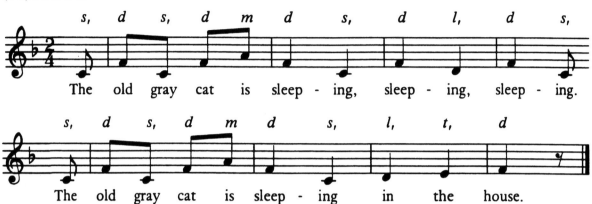

The old gray cat is sleep - ing, sleep - ing, sleep - ing.

The old gray cat is sleep - ing in the house.

1 The old gray cat is sleeping in the house.

  – the cat sleeps in the middle; all the other children (the mice) watch and sing from "hiding" places.

2 The little mice are creeping.

  – the mice creep on all fours around the kitchen, but not too close to the cat.

3 The little mice are nibbling.

  – the mice nibble on some pretend food; the cat stays asleep.

4 The little mice are sleeping.

  – the mice sleep after their big lunch; the cat stays asleep.

5 The old gray cat is prowling.

  – the cat wakens and prowls around on "all fours"; the mice stay asleep.

6 The little mice are scampering . . . . .

  – the mice scamper back to original "hiding" places. The cat tries to touch some.

The game can be repeated with several cats. Young children become caught up in this drama and forget to sing. Repeat at the end, with a "concert version" of the drama. The children sing the story and "finger play" the actions.

All the little ducklings

(3-4) l s f m r d

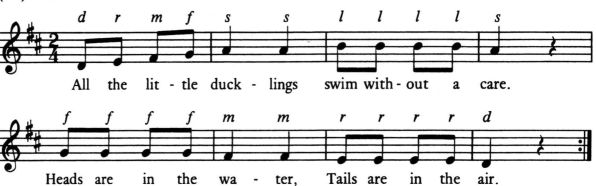

All the lit - tle duck - lings swim with - out a care.

Heads are in the wa - ter, Tails are in the air.

Formation: All can participate. Sit in a good space.
Line 1. Children all squat and "waddle" forward like ducks.
Line 2. Follow words – heads down and tails up.

This is another small drama that can be repeated several times as above. It is good to end with a "finger play" version so that the children can sing the whole song, in line 2 the "acting" takes precedence over the singing, usually.
Line 1. "paddle" fingers along legs
Line 2. on "heads", turn hands over
       on "tails", point fingers up straight.

Punchinello

(4-5-6) l s f m r d

1. What can you do Pun - chi - nel - lo fun - ny fel - low?
2. We'll do it too, Pun - chi - nel - lo fun - ny fel - low.

What can you do Pun - chi - nel - lo fun - ny clown?
We'll do it too, Pun - chi - nel - lo fun - ny clown.

Formation: stationary circle, standing.

Game: choose the clown with a counting out game.

Verse 1 – Punchinello, the clown, stands in the middle of the circle. The clown improvises a repeated motion with head, arms, legs or whole body. Try to match the beat and tempo of the singing with the clown's action – it could be different with each repetition. Punchinello chooses the next clown. Repeat till all have had a turn.

Rule: each child must choose a different action.

Skip one window

(3-4-5) l s f m r d

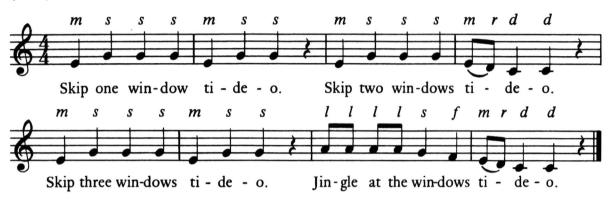

Formation: Stationary circle with spaces between children for windows.

Equipment: One or two jingle bells (3 or 4 bells fastened to a small strap).

Game: Choose a "jingler" with a counting-out rhyme. This child skips or gallops, holding jingle bells in one or both hands, in and out the "windows". On the word "jingle", the skipping child stands in front of a second child, and jingles the bells for the last phrase of the song. The second child is given bells by the first child, and becomes the new jingler-skipper. Repeat until all have had a turn.

Let's take a walk

(5-6) l s f m r d

Let's take a walk, take a walk, take a walk. To see what we can see now.

Formation: When the children can step on the beat and are ready to move as a group, they are ready to try this game. The children stand along a wall, *holding hands*.

Game 1. The teacher holds the first child's hand and asks all to watch and follow "so we can sing and walk in a long line". Turn your face and your body a little, so you can see where to go. Keep holding hands and let's "see what we can see".

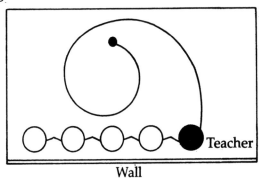

Down the road

(4-7) m r d l s

D. J. W.

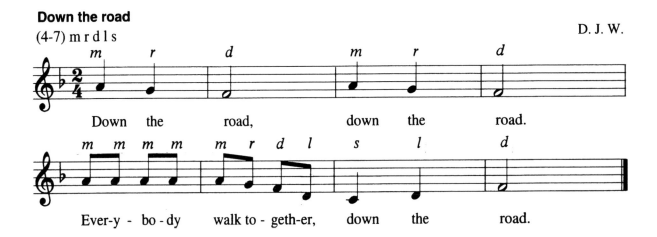

Down the road, down the road. Ever-y - bo - dy walk to - geth-er, down the road.

Game 2. Make a "snail". The teacher continues walking into the (1) circle, like a spiral. Then the teacher (2) turns and "unwinds" the spiral and the group finds itself in a long line again. Try other patterns. Is there a child that is ready to lead the line?

Photo: Dave Hill

All around the buttercup

(5) s m r d

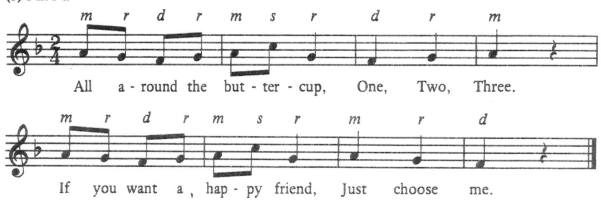

All a-round the but-ter-cup, One, Two, Three.

If you want a hap-py friend, Just choose me.

Formation: Moving circle, holding hands. Choose a child to be the buttercup.
Game: "Buttercup" stands in the centre. The children in the circle hold hands, turn body and face in direction circle is going, then step around the buttercup, on the beat. The "buttercup" chooses the next child to go to the centre.

Word game: Can you think of another *flower* that has three sounds (♪♪ ♩) to sing about? hyacinth
      – another bush? lilac bush
      – another leaf? maple leaf
      – another animal? crocodile, elephant
      – another insect? bumble bee
      – anything else? cuckoo clock

Sally go 'round the sun
(5) l s m r d

Sal - ly go 'round the sun,   Sal - ly go 'round the moon.

Sal - ly go 'round the chim - ney top,   ev - ery af - ter-noon. *Turn*
(spoken)

Formation: Moving circle, holding hands. Choose 3 children, a sun, a moon and a chimney to stand in the middle of the circle. Let the children decide how "to be" the sun, the moon and the chimney.

Game: Sing the song *twice* without stopping. The first time the children step around counter clockwise. On the spoken word TURN, the children turn their bodies to go in the opposite (clockwise) direction. The children can rest their hands while the sun, moon and chimney choose 3 new children for the centre of the circle.

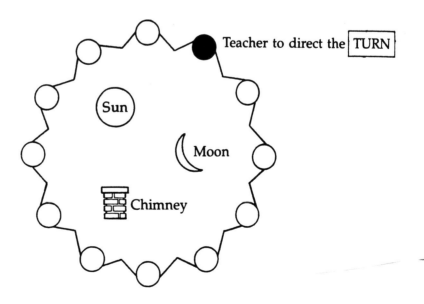

Who's that knocking at the door?

(5) s m r d

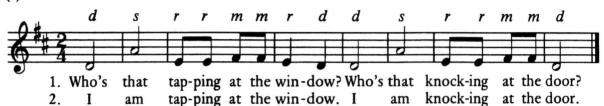

1. Who's that tap-ping at the win-dow? Who's that knock-ing at the door?
2. I am tap-ping at the win-dow. I am knock-ing at the door.

Formation: This is a voice identifying game. The children need to know each other quite well and they need to be able to sing the 2nd verse as a solo. Stationary circle. Choose a child to squat, with *eyes covered*, in the middle of the circle.

Game: Verse 1. The children all sing while the teacher **silently** points to one of them. This child goes in to the centre and "knocks" on the door.

Verse 2. The child who is "knocking on the door" sings this verse alone. At the end of the verse, the first child tries to identify who is "tapping on the window".

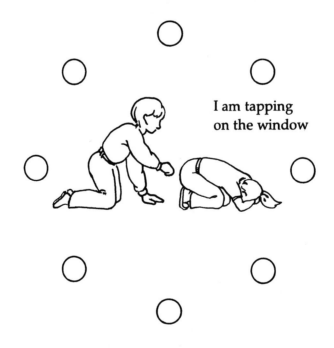

I am tapping
on the window

Hallowe'en is pumpkin time

(3-4-5) s f m r d

Lucile Panabaker

2. Hallowe'en is dress-up time etc.
3. Hallowe'en is candy time etc.

This rollicking melody sings itself! Encourage the children to *improvise* some other words about Hallowe'en. And what about Christmas? "Christmas time is Santa Claus, Ho! Ho! Ho!"
And what about Easter? "Easter time is easter eggs Yum! Yum! Yum! "This is a word-game song where the children's own ideas become part of the song, a valuable musical experience.
(5-yrs)
"Inner" hearing game: "Sing" the "Ho Ho Ho's" *inside* while *clapping* the rhythm pattern
(♩. ♩. ♩.).

I love little pussy

(4-5) s f m r d

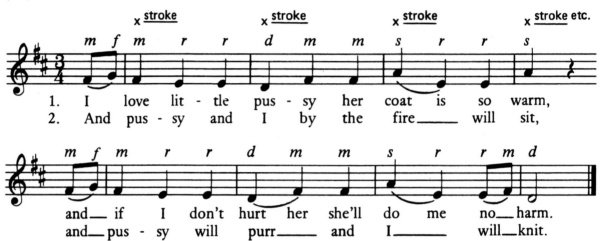

Finger play game: To feel $\frac{3}{4}$ metre.

The children sit in a space on the floor and hold one forearm up "to be" the pussy cat. With the other hand, they stroke their "pussy cats" with a long slow pat (from elbow to fingers). Change arms and repeat this song-finger play. Emphasize the $\frac{3}{4}$ metre in this finger play with a gentle accent on the 1st beat of the bar.

I sent a letter to my love

A game for Valentine's day

(3-4-5) f m r d t, l, s,

1. s, d d r m d m r s, d d r m d t,

I sent a let - ter to my love and on the way I dropped it.

2. s, d d r m f m r d t, s, l, t, d d

A lit - tle dog - gie picked it up and put it in his poc - ket.

Formation: Stationary standing circle. Choose "it".

Equipment: A small letter that would fit into a child's pocket.

Game: Phrase (1) "It" walks around the *outside* of the circle carrying the letter and drops it on the floor behind another child, who becomes the "doggie".

Phrase (2) The "doggie" picks it up and puts it in his or her pocket (substitute a sleeve, or waist band if necessary).

The first child joins the circle, but sits, so that all will know who has had a turn. The doggie becomes "it" and the game proceeds from the beginning until all have had a turn.

concept:
phrase feeling

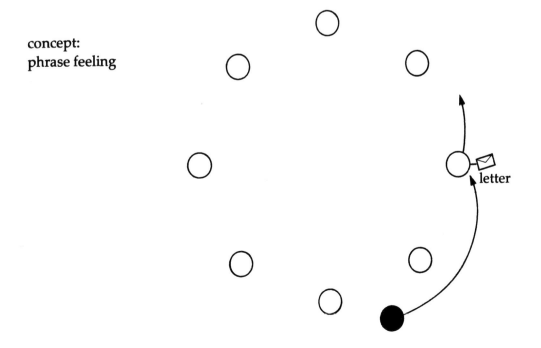

Down came a lady

(5-6) m d l, s,

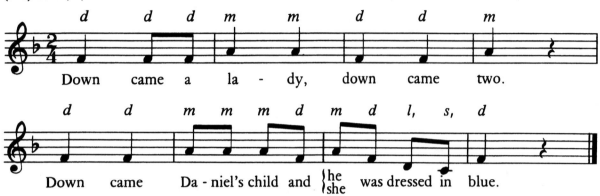

Down came a la - dy, down came two.

Down came Da - niel's child and {he/she} was dressed in blue.

Formation: A moving circle, holding hands. Choose a "lady".

Game: The circle, holding hands, steps around *counter clockwise*. The "lady" steps around *outside* the circle, *clockwise*. On Daniel's child, the "lady" touches a circle-child on the back. This child leaves the circle and joins the lady, stepping around behind her, holding hands. Repeat. At each repetition, the "lady-line" gets longer and the circle gets smaller until all are chosen. The children find this an amazing development. It is good to follow this game with a quiet sitting game or a short relaxation period.

Suggestions: Instead of BLUE, sing the colour of the clothing of the "chosen" child. Instead of "Daniel's Child", sing the name of the child so that it will fit the rhythm pattern e.g. Billy Jones or Eleanor.

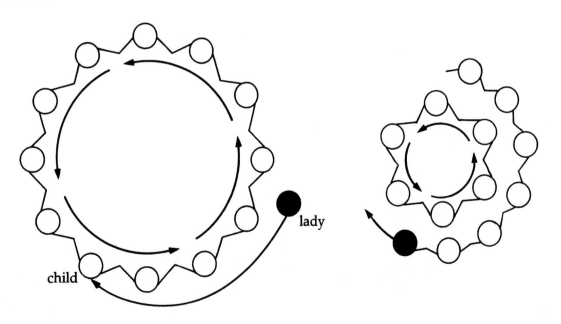

Here we go 'round the mountain − a partner game

(5-6) s f m r d

1. Here we go 'round the moun - tain two by two.
2. Show - a pret - ty mo - tion two by two.

Here we go 'round the moun - tain two by two.
Show - a pret - ty mo - tion two by two.

Here we go 'round the moun - tain two by two.
Show - a pret - ty mo - tion two by two.

Rise_____ su - gar rise.

Formation: Children choose partners; count the number of couples.

Teacher makes a circle on the floor with *different coloured* markers, one for each couple. Each couple stands outside the marker circle, facing counter clockwise. One couple steps into middle, crouching or kneeling.

Equipment: Different coloured markers (bean bags, tiles, cardboard squares etc.).

Game: Verse (1) Partners circle around centre couple, gauging steps so that they arrive back at their marker before end of verse. Centre couple "rises" on last phrase.

Verse (2) Centre couple improvises a motion, and all couples imitate it. Before going back to their own marker, the centre couple chooses next couple to go to the centre.

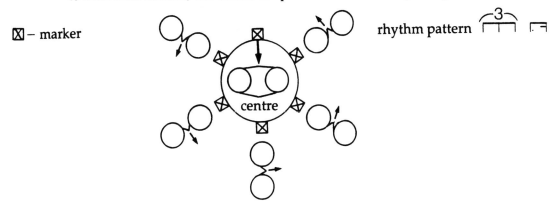

☒ − marker   rhythm pattern

Five little robins

(3-4-5) l s f m r d

Five / Four / Three lit - tle rob - ins sit - ting in a row, ... says

"cheep! cheep! I must go." One lit - tle, two lit - tle,

three lit - tle, four lit - tle, five lit - tle ro - bins go.

Formation: Children sitting in a row, backs to the wall. Decide where "home" is to be − on other side of room.

Game: Count the number of "robins" so that the children will know the appropriate number to sing. On bar 5, the teacher and the children sing the name of the child that is to fly home. That child flys around room and tries to come home by the end of the music. As listening skills develop, some children will "land" on the last word "go". The game ends when all the birds are "home".

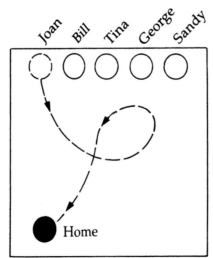

Skills: To feel exactly when the last note comes.

Singing a sequence in bars 7, 8 and 9. Show it with hand levels.

The farmer's in the dell

(4-5) l s f m r d

1. The far - mer's in the dell, the far - mer's in the dell.

Hi ho the der - ry oh, the far - mer's in the dell.

2. The farmer takes a wife.
3. The wife takes a child.
4. The child takes a nurse.
5. The nurse takes a dog.
6. The dog takes a cat.
7. The cat takes a rat.
8. The rat takes the cheese.
9. The cheese stands still.

Formation: Standing circle; "pick up" beat (♩.) with stamps, claps, or patchen. The game, as written, requires 8 different characters. So that all can participate if there are more than 8 children, the rat could take more "cheeses" so that *all* are in the middle at the end of the game.

Game: Choose the farmer with a "counting out" game. He or she stands in the middle. Each character chooses another child to come into the middle at the beginning of each verse. On verse 9, all children clap hands above heads, on the beat.

Here we go looby loo

(3-4-5) l s f m r d

Chorus

Here we go loo - by loo,   here we go loo - by light.

Here we go loo - by loo,   all on a Sa - tur-day night.

Verse

1. You put your right hand in,   you take your right hand out.

You give your hand   a shake, shake, shake and turn your-self   a - bout.

2. You put your left hand in.
3. You put your right foot in.
4. You put your left foot in.
5. You put your head right in.
6. You put your whole self in. (just ONE step)

Formation: A stationary, standing circle. A dramatic introduction adds interest — the circle is a bath, ready for Saturday night. When you put your hand "in", the water is very hot, so you quickly take it out again, as the song tells you.

Game: Chorus, pick up the beat with clap, stamp, patchen, or finger snap.

　　　Verse, action follows words.

The big ship sails down the Allee-Allee-O

(5-6) m r d t, l, s,

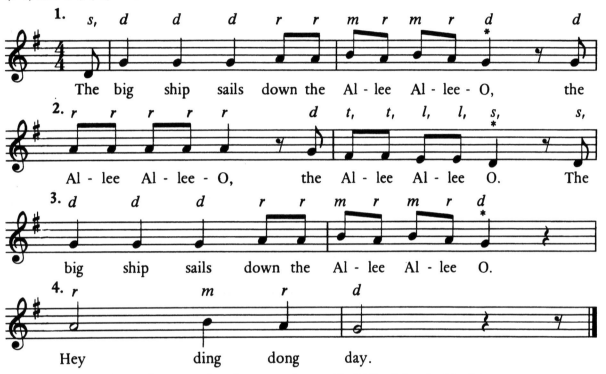

Formation: Two lines, facing each other to make a *wide* "Allee" for the *big* ship.

The partner games on page 53 prepare the children for the "allee" formation and for walking, in couples, up and down.

Game: phrase (1) Top couple hold hands and walks 7 steps *up* the allee.

        (2) Top couple turns and walks 7 steps *down* the allee.

        (3) Top couple turns and walks 7 steps *up* the allee.

        (4) Top couple separates and goes to new places in the lines at the bottom of the allee.

All children sing and clap the beat for the first 3 phrases. On phrase (4) clap the rhythm pattern while singing. Note: the "allee" will move down the room as the game progresses so make allowance for this.

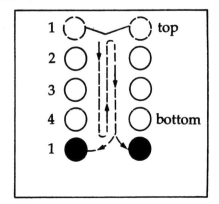

Feel the phrase length by walking exactly 7 steps. A signal on the triangle at * makes this very clear.

Tommy thumb

(3-4-5) l s f m r d

A finger play that can develop into an individual movement game.

2. Peter Pointer up.

3. Toby Tallman up.

4. Ruby Ringman up.

5. Baby Finger up.

6. Finger Family up.

When the children know this finger play, then continue the game as follows —

Line A — Sing each child's name in turn to dance (or skip or walk)

Line B — Soloist continues while the other children all sing and clap on the beat.

For a finale:

1) All the boys stand up, All the boys sit down etc.

2) All the girls stand up, All the girls sit down etc.

3) Everybody up, Everybody down etc.

See the ponies galloping

(2-3-4-5) s f m r d

Coleman and Thorne

See the po - nies gal - lop - ing, gal - lop - ing, down the coun - try road.

See the po - nies com - ing home, all tired out, all tired out.

Formation: Stand in good spaces, over whole room.

Galloping rhythm

Quick – Slow

Game: Line 1 (repeated) Ponies gallop, all going the same way, *down* the road, while the teacher sings.

Line 2 – Turn and go back to your space very slowly. Teacher sings and children can join in for the slow part.

Suggestion: After playing the game several times, children can sit in their space and sing the song as a finger play. The hands show the quick tempo and then the slow tempo (two beats to a bar).

Song books

Birkenshaw, L. and Walden, D.: **The Goat With the Bright Red Socks** Berandol, 1980
Buck, Percy: **The Oxford Nursery Song Book** Oxford University Press, 1933
Choksy, L.: **The Kodaly Context** Prentice Hall, 1981
Forrai, K. and Sinor, J.: **Music In Preschool** 1994 (2nd ed.)
Fowke, E.: **Sally Go Round the Sun** McClelland and Stewart, 1969
Seeger, R.C.: **American Folk Songs for Children** Doubleday, 1948

Student project

Analyse a song or singing game from a standard nursery school or kindergarten music book by considering some or all of the following criteria:

1 Do the children enjoy the song and can they sing all the words and the melody *without help* of teacher or accompanying instrument?

2 Is it a traditional nursery song, a genuine folk song or a composed song?

3 Does the text reflect the thought and language *of* young children? Do the actions reflect the natural movement of young children?

4 Indicate the meter, and write the rhythm pattern of the melody.

5 Compare rhythm pattern with text. Do they fit together in a natural and musical way?

6 State vocal range of melody and the pitch of the highest and lowest note.

7 Describe the melody i.e. starting note, scale step, leaps, ascending or descending, phrases and breathing places etc.

8 Mention any unique or interesting characteristics of the song.

9 What specific elements of music could the children experience in this song or singing game?

10 Evaluate the *artistic* value of this song. Would you teach it to your class? If not, why not?

Music learning through sound and listening games

Young children are as interested in random sounds in their environment as in organized musical sounds. Every teacher, at sometime, has to deviate from the lesson plan, when a fire engine goes by, or when a window rattles, or when the water pipes make a gurgling sound. When children play, they experiment with sounds using mouth, voice, tongue, hands or feet. They imitate and learn about sounds from their environment. This listening and experimenting with sound can lead to musical learning, if the parent or teacher is aware of the possibilities here.

"Where did that sound come from?"

"What is making that sound?"

"What is it made of? metal? wood?"

Too much sound is noise, an undesirable sound. Even music can be noise, if it is used inappropriately. Modern children live in a noisy world; they have learned to "turn off" their ears in self-protection. Most come to us needing special *listening games* to open their ears to the sounds of music.

Before we can teach music, we must teach the child to listen. Children with normal ears can hear, but can they listen? Listening means making a mental effort to understand what is heard.

But before playing listening games, the teacher must listen to the sound environment of the classroom. Is it conducive to listening and learning? Background music from radio, records or "piped-in" music is a form of noise pollution. It teaches children to "turn-off" their ears.

Music experiences with sound and listening games

Sound and listening games

Open your ears

1 Close your eyes and *listen!* Wait, and think for a minute.

       Billy, what do you hear? – "footsteps"

       Mary, what do you hear? – "the wind"

       Anna, what do you hear? – "a fire engine"

2 Close your eyes and *listen!*

       John, what am I doing to make this sound? (teacher claps hands)

       Peggy, what am I doing to make this sound? (teacher slides foot on floor)

       George, what am I doing to make this sound? (teacher snaps fingers)

3 Sound box toy

       Place a selection of interesting sounds in a toy box or a sturdy shoe box e.g. a small bell; a pair of sand paper blocks; 2 wooden stirring spoons; 2 metal spoons; several shakers made from spice boxes or jars, each containing a *different* "sounding" material such as rice, gravel, buttons, dried beans etc. – glue the lid on firmly! Encourage children to explore and experiment with these sounds.

4 Montessori Sound matching toys.

       Identical wooden cylinders with a sound inside. There are two of each sound. Children match "same sound" cylinders.

Sound and silence

1 *Walk* while I play the drum (piano, claves). *Stop* when the drum stops. Repeat several times. The children learn to stop *exactly* when the drum stops.

2 "Statues" or "freeze". *Run* while the drum runs (⊓ ⊓). Make a "statue" or "freeze" when the drum stops. Start with several phrases of regular length – then introduce longer or shorter phrases. Make a different statue, *each time* you "freeze".

Timbre – specific characteristics of sound

1 Collect a number of articles made of wood, unbreakable glass, metal, plastic, cardboard etc. Strike each with a small beater, so that the children will discover the sound differences of these articles. Place in a toy box so that individual children can tap and listen for sound differences.

2 Compare sounds of *four* percussion instruments (maraca, triangle, wood sticks, a drum with a "skin" head). What is each *made* of? What is the *name* of each instrument? Play each sound behind a screen. The children must tell the name of the instrument by *listening* to the *sound.*

3 Demonstrate and compare the timbre of melody instruments: the violin, the piano, a recorder, a glockenspiel, a xylophone.

4 Who said my name? Play this game when the children know each other's names. Prepare 4 cards (postcard size) [1] [2] [3] [4]. Ask 4 children to stand behind the screen (piano, drapery) and then give each child a numbered card.

    Teacher: "Number one, *say* my name"

    Child Number One: "Mrs. Wood".

    Teacher to group, "Who is number one, who *said* my name".

Continue until all 4 speaking voices have been identified. Repeat until all children have had a turn with a card behind the screen.

5 Who sang my name? Play as above but *sing* "s s m s s m" (Number one sing my name).
6 "Who's that knocking" is a more challenging voice identifying game p. 114.

When does the sound stop?
Children seated near the teacher.
Open your hands when I play a sound on the *cymbal*.
Close your hands when you hear the sound stop.
Try a triangle or the piano, with and without the damper pedal, for this game.

Point to the ceiling

Point to the ceiling, *Point* to the floor,

Point to the window, *Point* to the door.

Point to the table, *Point* to a chair,

Point to the teacher/mothers sitting over there,

Point to your head now, *Point* to your knee,

Point to your elbow, Now *Point* to me.

This *"Listen and Point"* Rhyme is a good introduction song for a *new* teacher in a *new* room with *new* children – a good moment to tell them your name, and ask the children to say their names. I suggest speaking the rhyme slowly and clearly with a *pause* at the commas when the children "point". It can be sung to the *"Baa Baa Black Sheep"* melody another time.

Where does the sound come from?

I The farmer's in the barn

1. The far - mer's in   the barn,   the far - mer's in   the barn,
2. The far - mer has   a cow,   the far - mer has   a cow,

hi   ho   the der - ry   oh,   the far - mer's in   the barn.
hi   ho   the der - ry   oh,   the far - mer has   a cow.

Formation: A circle in the middle of a *large* room. Choose the farmer.

Verse 1 The farmer's in the barn etc. (the farmer stands in the middle of circle)

Verse 2 The farmer has a cow etc. (the farmer chooses a cow to stand beside him)

Verse 3 The farmer has a duck etc. (the farmer chooses a duck to stand beside him)

Verse 4 The farmer goes to sleep etc. (lies down, hiding face) and the animals "hide" at opposite ends of room.

Verse 5 The farmer wakes up (stands up). The farmer calls out "Where is my cow" – the cow answers "moo" from hiding place. The farmer listens, then decides where to go to get the cow.

Verse 6 The farmer's found the cow etc. (farmer brings back cow to circle). the farmer calls out "Where is my duck" – continue as with cow.

Verse 7 The farmer's found the duck etc.

   Note: This game could be extended to include 4 farm animals.

Here is a variation of the game above, using the same melody.

II The leader has a band

The children need to know the name and the sound of the instruments. Choose 2-4 *percussion instruments* with contrasting sounds (in place of animals). The leader stands in the middle of circle with 2-4 instruments on the floor.

1 The leader has a band (leader waves arms like a conductor).

2 The leader has a drum (leader chooses a child to play the drum).

Continue as in farm game. The children learn to be comfortable holding an instrument and **not** make a sound until the correct moment.

Making sounds; sound and movement

Make a sound − make a different sound − listen to your sound.

1 What sounds can you make with your tongue, your teeth, your lips, your cheek?

2 Make a different clapping sound − with hollow hands, flat hands; one, two, three, or four fingers?

3 What other part of you can make a sound? stamp feet; pat legs; clap hands; snap fingers. . . .

4 What about your voice? − Speak, sing, whisper, hum.

5 Pictures and sounds − What does this picture say? Animals and birds in the city, on the farm, in the jungle or the zoo. Machines − a clock, a vacuum cleaner, a mixer. Transportation − a car, truck, aeroplane, boat, horse, motorcycle. Picture books with large clear illustrations will interest the children and give some structure to these "sound activities".

6 The sounds of nature.

> What does the wind say?
> What does the rain say?
> What does the sun say?

Nature, transportation, machine and animal sounds are a special joy to the children when combined with movement. An appropriate accompaniment on the piano or a percussion instrument controls the starting and stopping.

> What does the wind do?
> What does the rain do? ∕
> What does the sun do?

Listening games to teach the elements of music

Loud and soft (dynamics)

1 Say my name (use normal voice) — Mrs. Wood

Say my name with a loud voice — MRS. WOOD

Say my name with a soft voice — Mrs. Wood

Continue with: *Sing* my name ... (normal; louder; softer). *Play* the drum ... (normal; louder; softer).

Maintain a moderate tempo for this element. Children tend to alter the tempo for "loud" and "soft". This is not valid, musically speaking. It is better to focus on one element at a time. Later, two elements can be combined.

"Sing softly *and* quickly"

"Play your instrument loudly *and* slowly"

2 Add variety and interest to rhymes and songs by changing the dynamics, when repeated.

3 Some songs have "built-in" changes. Frère Jacques is a good example. Sing the first two lines *softly* and the last two lines *loudly*. Ask the children to choose appropriate instruments to accompany this song.

4 After a loud marching song, sing a lullaby. Pin-point the difference.

Fast and slow (tempo)

Children enjoy the metronome. They like to watch it, clap with it, and walk with it.

1 Metronome Game

Set the metronome at ♩ = 88 (a moderate tempo)

"Listen and clap with the metronome".

Set the metronome at ♩ = 120 (a faster tempo)

"Listen and clap *quickly* with the metronome" — clap quietly.

Set the metronome at ♩ = 60 (a slower tempo)

"Listen and clap *slowly* with the metronome".

Point out that you have to clap *differently* — for *quickly*, a very small motion, and for *slowly*, a larger motion.

2 Sing well-known songs at faster and slower tempi using body percussion to keep the beat.

3 Play percussion instruments at several tempi with the teacher keeping the beat with a drum or the piano.

High and low (pitch)

1 Prepare with movement games p. 55; aeroplane game p. 144

2 Prepare with voice sounds

"Be a cow with a low voice; walk and "moo" like a cow".

"Be a bird with a high voice; fly and "tweet" like a bird".

The teacher accompanies with high and low sounding percussion instruments (drum, triangle) or use the piano.

"When I play low sounds, be a cow; when I play high sounds be a bird. Listen so you will know what to be".

3 Prepare with speech

　　Say my name with a high voice.

　　Say my name with a low voice.

Use other words and rhymes that clearly reinforce the concept of high and low sounds.

4 Introduce three pitches with the story of the Three Bears – Father bear with a *low* voice; Mother bear with a *middle* voice; and Baby bear with a *high* voice. First the teacher, and then three children can speak in low, middle and high voices as they say

　　"Someone's been sitting in my chair" . . .

　　"Someone's been eating my porridge" . . .

　　"Someone's been sleeping in my bed" . . .

5 Place high sounds and low sounds in the sound box toy (p. 130). Ask the children to listen and tell which sounds are high and which are low.

6 Play a drum, a 5" cymbal with a beater, and a triangle. Which sound is high? Which is low? What would you say about the other one? (the cymbal) Yes, it's a sound in the middle.

7 Show the range of an octave with hand levels.

Play a high sound (C')on the piano (recorder, xylophone) teacher's voice.

　　"Hold your hands up *high* when you hear a *high* sound".

Play a low sound middle C on the piano (recorder, xylophone).

　　"Hold your hands down *low* when you hear a *low* sound".

Play slowly, so that the children will have time to listen and to respond physically to "high" and "low".

After several sequences of high-low, introduce the *same* sound.

e.g. C'-C'-C'　　　C-C-C　　　C'-C'-C-C-C'　　　C-C'

Now introduce a middle sound

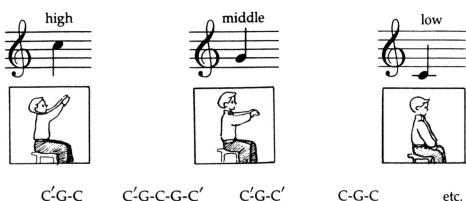

C'-G-C　　　C'-G-C　　　C'-G-C-G-C'　　　C'-G-C'　　　C-G-C　　　etc.

8 Play the preceding game with a *glockenspiel*, held in a *vertical* position so that the high sounds are at the top. The children show the pitch with hand levels while the teacher slowly plays or sings – high-low (C'-C), high-middle-low (C'-G-C). Hide the glockenspiel behind a screen. Can the children show high, middle and low pitches?

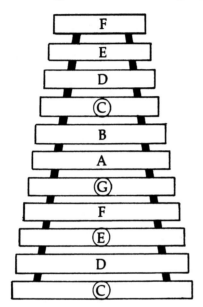

Children show pitch with hand *levels*

(1) High – low

(2) High – middle – low

(3) High – middle – down a little – low

(4) Low – up a little – middle – high

(5) Same sound C'C'C'C' d' d' d' d'
      G G G G s s s s
      E E E E m m m m
      C C C C d d d d

This game prepares the children, subconsciously, for reading and writing music on the staff.

The children will want to hear and play the other glockenspiel-sounds, so a "scale game" can be introduced now.

9 Ladder game

Show me how you climb up a ladder. Go slowly and carefully, one step at a time (Teacher plays ascending scale slowly on the glockenspiel.) Now come down the ladder, very slowly and carefully. When sounds go higher and lower like a ladder, we call this music a *scale*.

Scale song – pussy willow

I know a lit-tle pus-sy, Her coat is sil-ver gray, She

lives down in the mead-dow, not ve-ry far a-way. She'll

al-ways be a pus-sy, She'll ne-ver be a cat, For

she's a pus-sy wil-low. Now what do you think of that!

Meow   Meow   Meow   Meow   Meow   Meow   Meow   Meow   *SCAT (spoken)*

*Accent this note by playing the matching note on the glockenspiel.

If you have a real pussy willow, with just eight "buds", you can point to each bud and match it with the correct pitch as you sing the song. Children will follow your pointing, with "hand levels."

_____ what do you think of that?

_____ she's a pussy willow, Now

_____ never be a cat, For

_____ always be a pussy, She'll

_____ very far away. She'll

_____ lives down in the meadow, Not

_____ coat is silver gray, She

_____ I know a little pussy, Her

Start here Read up

Read down

Meow

Meow

Meow

Meow

Meow

Meow

Meow

Meow

SCAT (spoken)

137

Change the pitch

Sing well known songs, *with a small range,* at different pitches, changing not more than once or twice in each song. This is musically effective in a song or game with many repetitions or verses. If there are 8 verses, sing the first 4 in a lower key and the last 4 in a higher key.

Key of C

1. Ma - ry had a lit - tle lamb.

Key of F

4. It made the chil - dren laugh and play.

This makes an interesting musical development.

The teacher, without warning, leads into this key change with the singing voice, *so the teacher must have a good sense of pitch* and *inner hearing.* The children soon learn to "catch" and follow this key change.

Ring around a rosy (p. 101) does this in the 3rd verse.

"Hot Cross Buns" (p. 54) is a good song for this pitch change game.

Singing echo games

Tone matching

Start with the 2 or 3 note chant (s-m then l) and build in a developmental way up to a 5-6 note range. Omit semitones, at first, by using the pentatonic scale. Be sure the pitch is comfortable for the child — not too high or too low. Keep motives very simple until the children get the idea of an echo game.

Listen first — and *then* sing

my turn, point to yourself   your turn, point to children

A descending melody is easier; the falling minor 3rd is a natural interval for children — they use it in their play. Use *words* that interest the child with first echo games. Pick a theme to suit the moment and sing a series of different melodic progressions. Repeat a motive, once, if there are some "out-of tuners". Small motions with the hands help young singers, so use hand levels in space, to *show* the pitch.

Singing echoes require some preparation by the teacher. Ask the children for word and melody suggestions.

This type of listening game helps uncertain singers and also prepares children for playing on melody instruments (xylophone, piano etc.).

This singing echo or "copycat" game begins with the simplest motive – a falling minor 3rd (s m). The "copycat" song proceeds in developmental steps, ending on a 5 note descending scale pattern (s f m r d).

Adapt for other seasons:

I like autumn . . . coloured leaves are falling, etcetera.

I like winter . . . snow is in the garden, etcetera.

I like summer . . . playing in the playground, etcetera.

D.J.W.

Question and answer song

Who has the penny?

Formation: Circle, sitting down on the floor.

Equipment: A penny, a key, a thimble

Game: (1) Close your eyes and put your hands behind your back I will walk around the outside of the circle and I *may* put something in your hand (teacher quietly places penny, key and thimble in hands of 3 different children). Keep it a secret. We will ask you about it, with a singing voice.

(2) Open your eyes and listen to my singing question.

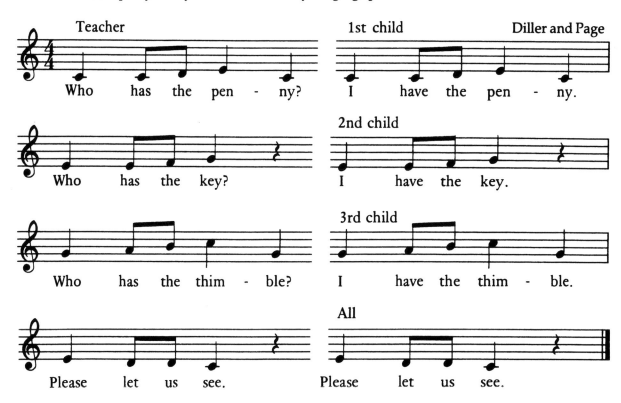

(3) Continue with the 3 "holders" of the penny, key and thimble, secretly placing them in the hands of 3 other children. Repeat until all have had a turn.

Many children's songs have phrases made from a motive followed by an echoing motive.

If this is pointed out and illustrated briefly to the children, it will help them remember the melody. We are then fostering the development of the child's *musical memory.*

Musical memory games

The words of a song are very important to the child. Therefore, much musical learning can be taught through singing in the early years. The words of a song help the child to remember the melody and the rhythm pattern. But if we are to develop the musical ear and also prepare the child for future instrumental music where there are no words, we should introduce some musical memory games *without words*.

1 What song is this?
The teacher "hums", "tra-la-las" or plays on the xylophone, a song well known to the children and with a distinctive melody or rhythm pattern. Some young children find this difficult at first. Then present the melody, only of the first phrase; the last phrase; the middle phrase;
2 Ask the children to hum or "tra-la" a well known song, without the words.
3 Point to the picture of the song I am humming (no words).

   etc.

Make picture cards which clearly show a feature or character of each song, learned from the beginning of the year. Which picture would you like to sing about, *by yourself*?
4 Sing well known songs with sounds (la, coo, bee etc.) instead of words. The children will become more aware of the shape of the melody line — where there is an echo motive; where the *same* sound is repeated; when the melody goes higher or lower.
5 Movement games starting on page 53 all stimulate the musical memory and listening skills.

Improvising with singing

This develops in the next stage of music education when voice skills are more secure, but a start can be made here.

Singing conversations and questions.

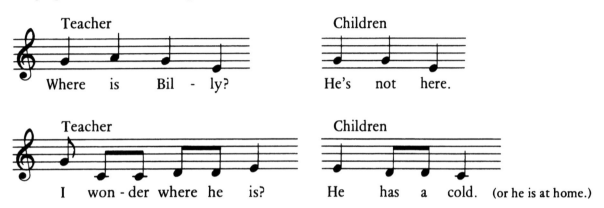

At first the child's response might be one word, which is a good start. Later, encourage the child to *sing* a short sentence response to give the feeling of a musical motive or phrase length.

"Sing a story about your dog..."

"Sing a story about a new toy..."

"Sing a story about ?..."

Improvising with words

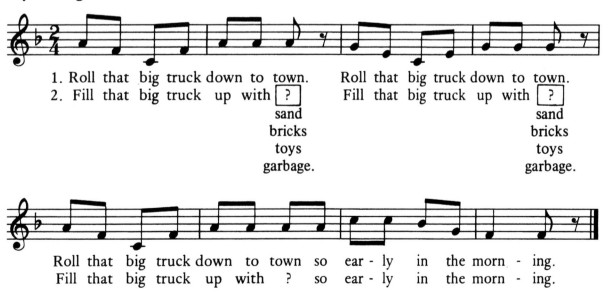

continue, giving each child an opportunity to suggest something to "fill that big truck".

Two song books which feature word improvisations:

American Folk Songs for Children by Ruth Crawford Seeger, Doubleday.

Music and Young Children by Frances Aronoff, Turning Wheel Press.

The aeroplane game (4-5-6 years)

The children kneel in good spaces. Use the whole room. One knee is on the floor and the other knee is bent, with the foot on the floor, ready "to push off". Arms are outspread, "like an aeroplane". Remind them that it is safer if all air planes fly around the room in the *same direction*. The children must be ready to run as a group and they must have learned to *listen to* and *follow* cues from the piano accompaniment. If the group is large, divide into two groups, with one group flying and other group parked on the runway.

Sound and movement suggestions · Piano accompaniment

a Airplanes stay in spaces; "warm up" engine making appropriate *mouth sounds – brrrrrr –*

b When the children hear the arpeggio motive going higher, they take off and fly (run) around the room, *all going the same way,* all making appropriate mouth sounds.

c Continue flying 5-10 seconds

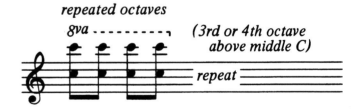

d When children *hear* arpeggio motive going down, they get *"ready to land"*.

e Land in starting position *when piano* sound stops.

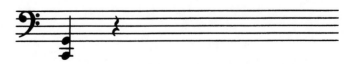

This is an exciting game for the children. But they must listen, move, and make a sound, *all at the same time.*

The firemen game (4-5-6)

Decide the location of the fire – perhaps a wall at the other end of the room. The firemen get ready to go. Divide group in half, if the group is large.

suggested sound and movement

suggested piano accompaniment

a The firemen drive the fire engines (run) around the room, making *siren sounds. When the music stops*, the firemen stop the engines and get out.

b The firemen take hoses from the fire engine and pour water on the fire, making hose sounds sssh   sssh
sssh   sssh   sssh
The fire is out when the piano sounds stop.

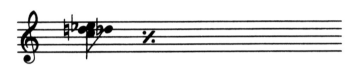

c The firemen have put the fire out, but they are tired and go back (walk) to the fire station *slowly*. The sirens are turned off.

Further reading

Caplan, T. and F.: **The Early Childhood Years: The 2 To 6 Year Old** Bantam, 1983
Schafer, R.M.: **Ear Cleaning** Berandol, 1969
        The Tuning of the World McClelland & Stewart, 1980

Listening books for children

Astrop, C. and J.: **Chatterbooks: Senses: Hear** St. Johns Breakwater, 1991
Hearn, E.: **Woosh! I Hear A Sound** Annick Press, 1983
Littler, Angela: **What Can You Hear?** Englewood Cliffs, Messmer, 1988
Parramon J. and Puig J.: **Sound** Barron, New York, 1986
Scarry, Richard: **Splish Splash Sounds** Western, N.Y., 1986
Showers P.: **The Listening Walk** Crowell, N.Y., 1961
Spier, P.: **Gobble, Growl, Grunt** Doubleday, N.Y., 1971
Stecher, M. and Randall, A.: **Max the Music Maker** Lothrop, N.Y., 1986

Student project
1 What could you do to improve the sound environment for your children – in your home; your nursery school; your music room; your day care centre; your kindergarten? Make a list.
2 Put together a "sound box" for a four year old child that has interesting timbres for young ears and is safe for young hands.

The special appeal of instruments

Beating a drum or jingling a bell is an appealing way for the young child to make music. Some children do not feel free to *move* with music at first; others have not *found* their singing voices. These children may participate joyfully with a simple percussion instrument and from this starting point, the teacher may entice them to venture into other ways of experiencing music.

Making music with percussion

First experiences: Free experimentation

Suggestions

1 Plan first experiences with care.
2 Introduce children to the world of music with a basket of child-safe, good-sounding instruments.
3 Select two sounds, to explore and experiment (jingle bells, small shakers).
4 First instruments must be comfortable for children to hold, and easy to play.
5 There must be at least one instrument for each child.
6 They must look attractive and sound well, even when all the children in the group are exploring and experimenting together e.g. for 12 children I would choose 6-8 jingle bells with handles and 6-8 small "child-sized" shakers.

two sounds

7 Each child chooses an instrument, tries it and discovers its sound quality. Try the other kind –
8 After some minutes of experimenting, the whole group could sing a well known song such as "Jingle Bells" or "Twinkle, Twinkle Little Star" with instruments, to give them the idea of playing and singing together. The singing words help the children feel the *beat* or *pulse*, and also the *beginning* and the *end* of the music.
9 Now, *play* and *sing* and *walk* with your instruments like a marching band or a parade. The teacher could provide support and control with a drum, a guitar, a recorder or the piano.
10 First instrument experiences should be short and happy. Walk among the children with the basket to collect the instruments, so that "they will be ready for another time".
11 Some words about being careful with these *special toys* would be appropriate at this first experience.
12 But, do not make children feel guilty, if they accidentally drop an instrument. Ignore it if possible, or help if necessary.

Some first instruments
Basic techniques and musical use

1 Introduce *one sound* at a time (i.e. jingles) with all the children playing the *same* instrument. The sound will have more meaning to the children. They can master the technique and therefore "make music" with the instrument. Later, more sounds should be added but four "sounds" are enough – metal (bell), shaker (maraca), wood (rhythm sticks), skin (drum). For a class of 12 children, I would suggest buying 12-14 of each sound. *Store each sound in a separate sturdy box.* It is common practice in nursery schools and kindergartens, to throw a random mix of instruments into the same container, which shows a lack of sensitivity to the qualities of sound. As with other equipment and toys, keep them *clean* and in *good repair*. Never give a child a broken instrument.

2 Place instruments on a large tray which the teacher can "bring out", or lay the instruments on a low table, ready for the children.

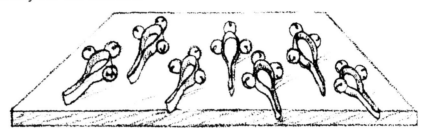

"Leslie, come and choose an instrument. Take it back to your place. Try it! What kind of a sound do you hear?"

3 Allow some minutes of "experimenting" and "exploring". Give help with technique and talk a little about sound quality and different effects with the instrument (bells can be shaken freely *or* one tapped on the other hand).

4 When all have an instrument, sing a well known song while playing together, trying to catch their beat – though this may take several experiences. Try another song, but first experiences should be short. A well-known song tells the children when to *start* and when to *stop*.

5 Ask each child to return instrument to the table.

6 Dynamics and tempo can be varied by choosing songs that are loud, soft, quick or slow.

7 Children will learn self discipline with instruments. "When you are ready, you may choose an instrument". "I will have to hold your instrument if you

- put it in your mouth
- bang it on the floor
- hit Leslie with it"

Take it immediately – return it to the child within a minute – *quietly* but *firmly*.

8 Some children will try to play two instruments at the same time i.e. beat the drum with a maraca. This causes instrument breakage, "sound" confusion and muddled technique. One at a time is more musical. Good instruments are expensive, so treat them with care.

Jingle bells

Bells can be shaken quickly or tapped on the other outstretched hand, to emphasize the pulse or the rhythm pattern

1 With speech: 1, 2, 3, 4, Jingle at the cot-tage door

    5, 6, 7, 8, Jingle at the gar-den gate.

2 Game songs with bells

  Bell horses – page 94

  Jingle bells – an all time favorite

  Skip one window – page 110

3 Add a different quality to basic movements by suggesting that the child carry a bell – walk, skip, jump, gallop or dance with bells.

4 Rhythm patterns

bells – ⊓ ⏐ ⊓ ⏐ ⋋ repeat softly

say – Jingle Bells Jingle Bells

bells – ⊓ ⊓ ⏐ ⏐ ⊓ ⏐ ⏐

sing – Jingle at the window ti-i-de-oh

Look for short speech patterns, rhymes, games and songs that are effective with jingle bells.

Maracas/Shakers

Small commercial ones are available. Heavy commercial ones are *not* suitable. Like bells, they can be shaken quickly or tapped on the hand. *One* maraca for each child is best. The traditional use, with a maraca in each hand, makes unnecessary complications for young children and the teacher. See page 168 for homemade shakers that make a good sound.

1 Rhythm with spoken rhyme

⏐ ⏐ ⏐ ⊓ ⏐ ⏐ ⏐

Cow-boy Joe went to Mex-i-co.

2 With movement

Walk, skip, jump, dance freely in a good space with a maraca.

3 Dance song with maracas

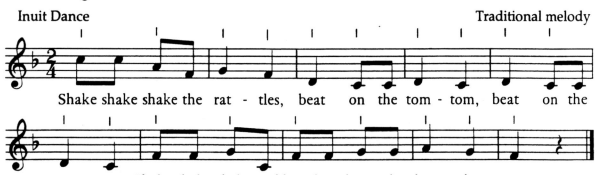

Children stand in good spaces. "Glue your feet to the floor; bend your knees a little on the beat, while you shake your rattles and sing.. The teacher sings and accompanies dance on a drum (tom tom). The children play on the beat, helped by the "knee-bend" movement. Some will pick up the rhythm pattern from the words.

4 Rhythm pattern in $\frac{3}{4}$ meter

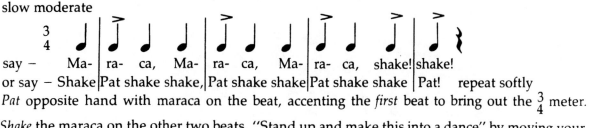

Pat opposite hand with maraca on the beat, accenting the *first* beat to bring out the $\frac{3}{4}$ meter.

Shake the maraca on the other two beats. "Stand up and make this into a dance" by moving your feet in your space, while you play the maraca.

Jingle hammers: A substitute for maracas. They are sturdier, but have a different sound.

Drums, Tom tom

This is a favorite way for young children to make music. The child sits on the floor and places the tom tom between outstretched legs. I believe that curved hands are the best beaters for first drumming experiences, so that the child can "feel" the sound as well as hear it. Indian tom toms made by native craftsmen make a pleasant soft sound and are suitable for a group of young children. The heads are of *soft suede* and are laced together. They can be purchased in souvenir gift shops. Try to have one for each child or, two children could take turns. They are easy to make with round metal tins 6" x 8". Remove both metal ends and lace on the heads. Pull the laces *tight* and tie securely.

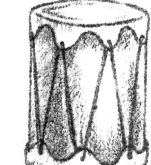

Note: 2 litre yogurt containers, turned upside down, make a good sound. When they are stacked together, they take up much less storage space than tom tom drums and are much less expensive.

First experiences should be exploring and experimenting, using both hands simultaneously. It takes time to acquire the technique of "lifting" the sound out of the drum head with a quick staccato movement. Curve the hand so that the sound is made with the finger tips – a flat hand produces a poor sound. The elbows should be held *up* and *away* from the body.

Using the tom tom (floor drum)

1 The tom tom or floor drum is good to bring out the beat in music, so when the children are ready,
help them find the beat and keep it steady for a short spoken rhyme.

> | | | |
> Rum Tum Play the Drum
>
> | | | |
> Rum Tum Stop the Drum

2 Sing and play
Start with songs in $\frac{2}{4}$ or $\frac{4}{4}$ meter, playing on the beat.

> Baa Baa Blacksheep
> Frère Jacques
> Yankee Doodle
> London Bridge

$\frac{6}{8}$ meter requires a slower, two to the bar, beat.

This is the way we play the drum   Traditional melody

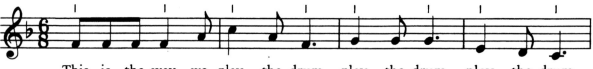

This is the way we play the drum, play the drum, play the drum.

This is the way we play the drum so ear - ly in___ the morn - ing.

Another $\frac{6}{8}$ melody that goes well with the drum is "Sally go round the sun".

3 Loud and soft drumming
With speech

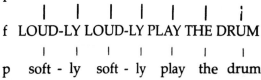

f LOUD-LY LOUD-LY PLAY THE DRUM

> | | | | | | |
> p soft - ly soft - ly play the drum

Sing and play songs twice, the first time *louder* and the second time *softer*. A piano accompaniment
can lead and control the dynamics (loud and soft). *Keep a steady beat.* Children tend to think that
loud also means *fast*- an incorrect concept, musically speaking!

4 Quick and slow drumming

Can you play *quickly* and *softly* at the same time. Keep your hands close to the drum when you play quickly.

Say and play

| | | | | | | |

Quick-ly Quick-ly play the drum

When you play slowly, use a bigger motion with your hands and arms.

| | | | | | | |

Slow- ly Slow- ly play the drum

5 Rhythm patterns with the drum

♩ ♩ ♫ ♩

One Two Tie my shoe

♩ ♩ ♫ ♩

Three Four Shut the door

Say your name on your drum

♩ ♩   ♫ ♩   ♩   ♫♪

Kar-en   Jen-ni-fer   Ann   E-li-za-beth

♩ ♩   ♫ ♩   ♩   ♫ ♫

Pat-rick   Ti-mo-thy   John   A-lex-an-der

See "name games with pictures" p. 77-80.

Playing the drum with a beater

A beater adds interest and a different sound to drumming. Buy sturdy beaters at a music supply store. Round, hard rubber type heads sound well, but be sure they are all well glued on. The stick should be about 9 inches long to be comfortable for the young child. One beater is enough for a beginner but ask the children to change the beater from one hand to the other, occasionally. Then both hands and arms will develop the technique and be ready for two beater drumming at a later time. Show the children how to wrap the whole hand around the end of the beater. Hold elbows up and away from the body and sit up straight. All the drumming games on pages 154 and 155 can be played, using a beater.

Rhythm sticks

Rhythm sticks are made of painted or varnished hardwood about 6-9 inches long and ¹/₂ inch in diameter. Bamboo garden stakes cut in 9 inch lengths make good rhythm sticks, though they sometimes split. Most commercial rhythm sticks are 12 inches long! Cut them in half and sand paper the rough ends. You will double your rhythm stick collection.

Hold rhythm sticks firmly in each hand with the complete hand curled around the end. Do not point the second finger along the stick. Raise elbows away from the sides of the body. To get a good clear musical sound, tap the end of one stick on the other stationary stick. *Quick* rhythms require a *small* motion. *Slow* beats require a *larger* motion.

They are excellent for keeping the beat and for tapping rhythm patterns.

Games:

1 Say and play the beat

| | | | | | | | | |

Tick Tock Says the clock Tick Tock stop

    (1) Be a *loud* clock (2) Be a *quiet* clock

2 Say and play rhythm pattern of animal names (see page 77)

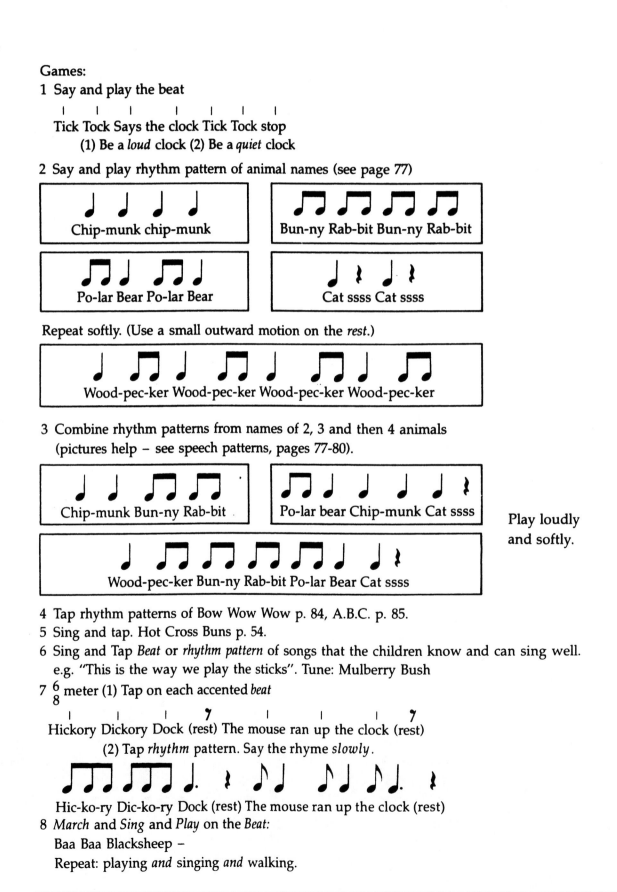

Repeat softly. (Use a small outward motion on the *rest*.)

3 Combine rhythm patterns from names of 2, 3 and then 4 animals
   (pictures help – see speech patterns, pages 77-80).

Play loudly
and softly.

4 Tap rhythm patterns of Bow Wow Wow p. 84, A.B.C. p. 85.

5 Sing and tap. Hot Cross Buns p. 54.

6 Sing and Tap *Beat* or *rhythm pattern* of songs that the children know and can sing well.
   e.g. "This is the way we play the sticks". Tune: Mulberry Bush

7 $\frac{6}{8}$ meter (1) Tap on each accented *beat*

| | | �7 | | | �7

Hickory Dickory Dock (rest) The mouse ran up the clock (rest)

    (2) Tap *rhythm* pattern. Say the rhyme *slowly*.

Hic-ko-ry Dic-ko-ry Dock (rest) The mouse ran up the clock (rest)

8 *March* and *Sing* and *Play* on the *Beat*:

Baa Baa Blacksheep –

Repeat: playing *and* singing *and* walking.

Hand drums

These require more technique.

They have a shallow wooden rim with a membrane or plastic head. They should be 6-8 inches in diameter for young children. Good ones have a small wooden "handle" inside the rim, making it easier for the child to hold it firmly. Some have a small finger *hole* and are *not* recommended. Young children get their fingers twisted or stuck in the hole. The child holds the drum about chest height with the head of the drum *vertical* to the floor. Keep the drum in this position. The other hand is the "beater". Lift the sound out of the drum with a quick "staccato" movement.

The beating hand should be curved so that the "cushions" of the fingers strike the drum. For special effect, finger tips, finger nails, a light weight mallet or a snare drum brush can be used. The drum can also be brushed with the hand to give wind or surf sounds.

Hand drum games

All the games suggested for floor drums are effective with hand drums. Hand drums are excellent to play and move around the room. These are very useful instruments and there should be one for each child in the class.

Games with different sounds − combining sounds

When the children have had some experience with jingles, maracas, drums and rhythm sticks, introduce games which make use of 2, 3 or 4 different sounds. Place some of each instrument you wish to use, on a low table − so that each child can choose one.

Games

1 (a) High Sounds and Low Sounds with Bells and Drums
The children choose bells or drums from a low table. The teacher plays the piano. "When I play "Baa Baa Blacksheep" with high sounds, on the piano, the bells play with me and the drums are quiet". "When I play "Baa Baa Blacksheep" with low sounds on the piano, the drums play with me and the bells are quiet".
"Listen, I might change in the middle of the song".
(b) Repeat with movement (teacher plays the piano)
High sounds − the bells walk and play; the drums stand still and wait for low sounds.
Low sounds − the drums walk and play; the bells stand still and wait for high sounds.
(c) Older children can learn to identify sounds in the "middle". "When I play in the middle, the rhythm sticks and/or the maracas play." Add this idea to above game.

2 Play and Sing and Move.
Baa Baa, Frère Jacques, Yankee Doodle and London Bridge, well known children's songs with a strong marching beat, go well with instruments. Encourage the children to *play* and *sing* and then to *play* and *sing* and *move*.

3 Copycat and games with instruments (Rhythm Echoes)
The teacher plays a drum or sticks and says

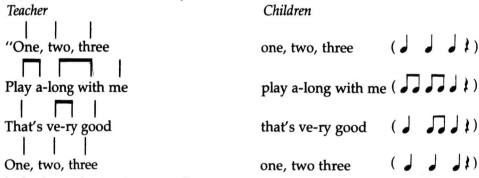

Continue with rhythms of animal names, flower names, etc. starting with short echo motives and gradually make them into a longer phrase length by adding more names.

4 The orchestra, with solo instruments   Lucile Panabaker

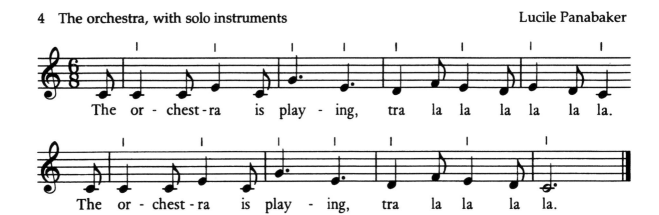

The or - chest - ra   is   play - ing,   tra   la   la   la   la   la   la.

The or - chest - ra   is   play - ing,   tra   la   la   la   la.

Drums only	2 The little drums are playing tra la la . . . (drums alone)
Jingles only	3 The jingle bells are playing . . .
Maracas only	4 Maracas now are playing . . .
Sticks only	5 The rhythm sticks are playing. . .
All play	6 The orchestra is playing . . .
All play and march	7 The orchestra is marching . . .

Solo instruments

These include a timpani drum, a bongo drum, a triangle, a wood block, a tambourine, a cymbal, a pair of sand blocks and a castinet.

Be sure that they are the correct size and weight for young children so they will sound musical when played by them. They should be sturdy so that the children can experiment and listen to various effects. The span of attention of the whole group must be long enough so that all can have a turn. Some of these are expensive; some are large and would require special storage and room space.

These solo instruments can be combined with other instruments, but as they have a unique tone and timbre, I believe that the children will hear these qualities better in individual solo experiences.

The timpani drum

This is a child sized tunable drum with adjustable legs. The beater should have a large, soft head. The bottom of the drum must be open. The head should be 14" to give a good C sound for the key of C, or D for the key of D.

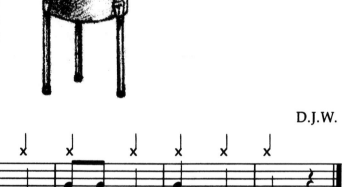

Drum song: tune drum to C   D.J.W.

Rum Tum play the drum. Rum Tum Tum.

The drum plays 4 "starting beats" as an introduction. Then the drummer and all the children sing the song. The drummer, then chooses the next drummer, until all have had a turn.

The drummer stands about 6 inches *away* from the drum. Hold the beater with complete hand wrapped around the end. Keep the elbow up and away from the body. Use the same staccato technique as for hand drums. Some children need to be reminded to "play with a medium sound", so that we can hear the singing voices. The children could sing all the songs they know with a drum introduction and accompaniment.

Bongo drum (child size)

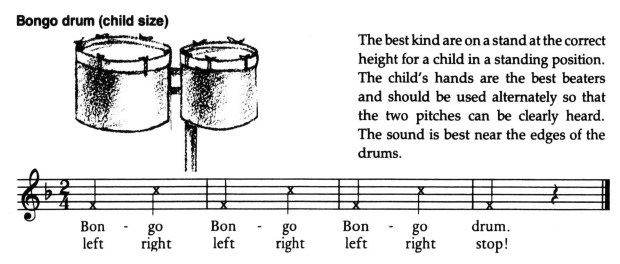

The best kind are on a stand at the correct height for a child in a standing position. The child's hands are the best beaters and should be used alternately so that the two pitches can be clearly heard. The sound is best near the edges of the drums.

| Bon | - | go | Bon | - | go | Bon | - | go | drum. |
| left | | right | left | | right | left | | right | stop! |

This accompaniment goes well with simple $\frac{2}{4}$ songs. The bongo prepares children for using both hands on barred instruments.

Triangle

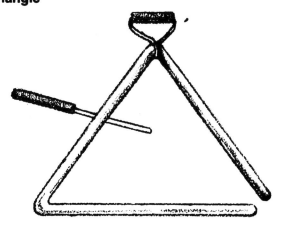

This is best kept for special sound effects. Its sharp ringing tone can dominate other sounds and voices, in an unmusical way. A large one, about 6", is easier for the child to manage. The holder should be carefully designed so that the triangle will not twirl around when played. The child's hooked index finger makes a better holder than a poorly designed string holder. Help each child to play *softly* and *lightly* on the closed side of the triangle, to get a musical sound.

"Jan, will you play the triangle softly while we all sing "Twinkle, twinkle, little star?" We will all make a "pretend" triangle with one hand and "play along" with Jan.

Tambourine

This can be tapped like a hand drum or shaken to add interest, but young children find it hard to control, sometimes. Use it for mysterious or scary sounds for Hallowe'en.

Sand block

These are rubbed together for special sound effects such as a train or water from a fireman's hose.

Cymbal

One 5" cymbal, played with a soft beater, for the last sound of a song, is effective and musical.

The triangle, tambourine, sand block and cymbal can be used effectively in timbre listening games (see pages 130, 131).

Castinet

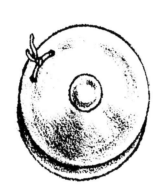

There are small inexpensive castinets that young children like to try. But they require a small muscle co-ordination in their hands, which may not be developed enough for rhythmical playing. They are good for sound and timbre listening games (page 130). When combined with maracas they make a fine authentic accompaniment to Spanish and Mexican folk songs and dances.

Wood block

Use a medium sized oblong one that can be held in the flat part of a child's outstretched hand, or a cylindrical one with a handle.

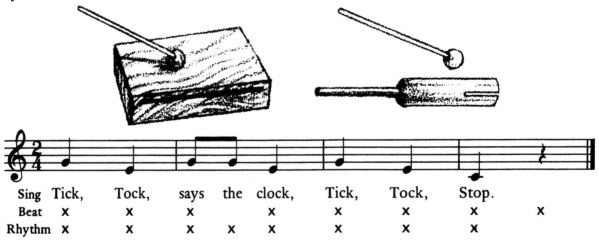

Sing	Tick,		Tock,		says	the	clock,	Tick,		Tock,		Stop.	
Beat	x		x	x		x	x	x	x	x
Rhythm	x		x	x	x	x	x	x	x	

One or several children sing and play. The other children sing and pretend to play. Pass the instruments around so all can have a turn. Try other "known" songs in $\frac{2}{4}$ meter. Teach the children how to sing and *play the beat* and also to sing and *play the rhythm*. They will need to know the difference.

Sound effects with instruments

Train – choo choo with sand blocks
Hallowe'en – tap or shake a tambourine
Mysterious slow sound – cymbal with beater
Horses feet – wood block or rhythm sticks
Clock striking – triangle
Woodpecker – rhythm sticks
Soldiers – drums

Be sure it has meaning *to the children*. When they get the idea, ask for suggestions for sound effects to go with movement, rhymes and songs.

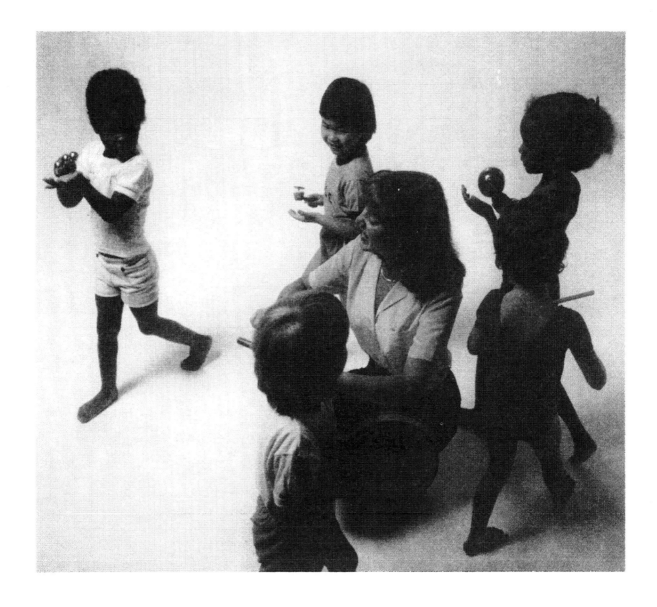

Melody instruments — tuned instruments

Chime bars

These instruments add a new musical dimension to the young child's experiences with percussion sounds. After some experience with basic percussion such as drums, sticks and jingles as well as listening and ear training games, they may be ready, at about four or five years of age, to play simple borduns to accompany their singing and also to play short melody patterns on melody instruments. These instruments require more physical co-ordination than the basic percussion instruments, and the child must be ready for some musical discipline. Singing is another pre-requisite. Chime bars offer a good introduction to the absolute pitch names of sounds C, D, E etc.

Chime bars — pentatonic scale

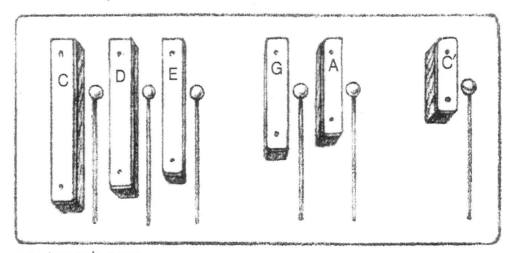

on a tray or in a case

I like to *demonstrate* the required technique to make a good sound on a chime bar *before* the children choose the sound they are going to play. By using the bars of the *pentatonic scale*, the children can all play together, while learning the technique. For 12 children, have 3 low C s, 3 G s, 3 high C's and one each of D,E and A.

The photograph shows the chimes on the floor in front of the children with hand and arm in a good position for playing the chimes.

Very *slowly* and *softly*, bounce the ball end of the beater on to the *middle* of the chime. Lift the sound "out of the instrument" with a short staccato movement using the *forearm and wrist*. Ask each child, one at a time, to choose a sound. Give each child a short practice time, before introducing the ensemble effect in "Ding Dong".

This "tone cluster" effect of all the sounds in the pentatonic scale playing together is musical if it is *slow* and *soft*. This "tone cluster" will accompany any C pentatonic song. Play on the beat.

The teacher can play and sing some "starting words" — the introduction. The children hold beaters about 4″ above chime, ready to play.

Rain rain go away

A. With poem interlude (in A B A form)

Children
sing

Children
play

Teacher plays
and sings

B. With speech interlude

Rain (Robert Louis Stevenson)

The rain is raining all around,
It falls on field and tree,
It rains on the umbrellas here,
And on the ships at sea.

Repeat A

Try "Ring around a Rosy" and "Engine Engine Number 9" with a C pentatonic "tone cluster".
    Tidy up: Who has a "D"? Play "D" while we sing D D D etc. Put D back on the tray.
Continue with other letter names.

Chime bar game

Children sit in *good spaces,* each with a chime bar and a beater. Teacher stands with timpani and a high C chime bar available with appropriate beaters, *one in each hand.*

1 When I play the chime bar ♩ ♩ ♩ ♩ , you sit and play your chime bar.

When I play the timpani ♩ ♫ ♩ ♫ ♩ , you stand up, *holding your beater,* and skip *around* your chime bar.

Start with 4 or 8 bar phrases, ending with a ♩ . Go directly to and from chime bar and timpani. Children must listen, react quickly and pick up the beat when playing the chime bar.

Playing melodies on chime bars

See Saw with G and E

See saw up and down, in the sky and on the ground.

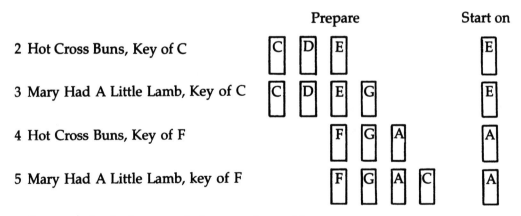

Ready now sing! play!

		Prepare			Start on
2 Hot Cross Buns, Key of C	C	D	E		E
3 Mary Had A Little Lamb, Key of C	C	D	E	G	E
4 Hot Cross Buns, Key of F	F	G	A		A
5 Mary Had A Little Lamb, key of F	F	G	A	C	A

Set out only the bars needed − on a low table.

Alto xylophone

This instrument has rosewood bars and a range from middle C to A'. The tone is dry and clear when played with felt tipped beaters.

The xylophone requires a quicker wrist action than chime bars. The instrument sits on the floor with the children kneeling on a small rug or pad in front; low C to the *left*.

1 Explore the sound range and learn to get a good sound. Use *both* hands. Show the children how to remove the bars, by lifting them up with a *hand on each side of the bar*. Show them how to put them on in the correct order. Can you read the letter names of the sounds? Which is the highest sound? Which is the lowest sound?

2 Remove F and B bars using both hands.
   "Walk" the mallets slowly on different bars, using alternate hands to make a melody. Say: walk, walk, walk, walk, as you play.

3 Play "two C's".
   Find low C and high C. Take all the other bars off, carefully. Play "two C's", both hands together, eight times. Be sure your elbows are away from your sides and you are holding the beaters correctly. The 2nd finger goes around the handle with the other fingers.
   This "two C" accompaniment goes with *any* simple song in the key of C. An introduction of 4 beats is a good idea, as in "Rain Rain" with chime bars (p. 165).

4 Playing melodies
   Play "See Saw" and "Mary had a little Lamb" and "Hot Cross Buns". Remove bars that are not needed for the song being played (see p. 166). Play each song several times. *Sing* while you play.

The metallophone (alto)

This instrument has a clear ringing quality. Show the children how to "damp" the sound at the end of the song. It goes well with the alto xylophone or can be played alone.

Other accompaniments for xylophone or metallophone.

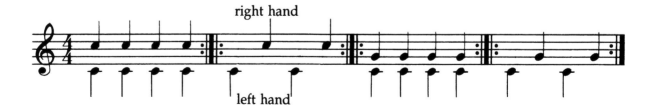

The children can make a start on these instruments by playing simple accompaniments, short scale step melodies, and simple explorations and improvisations.

They can also be used by a teacher who does not play the piano, for playing melodies, for finding the correct starting pitch of a song, and for high-low pitch games.

Buying instruments

Buy good quality, sturdy instruments for young children. Check for safety, sound and ease of handling by a child. If possible, try each instrument before you buy, or better still, see and hear a young child use it. Much can be done with 4 kinds of relatively inexpensive instruments – rhythm sticks, maracas, hand drums and jingles.

Instruments made by the teacher or parents

This is an inexpensive way to supplement the school's instrument collection. Books with instructions are available in libraries, teacher's supply stores and craft book stores. (see list p. 161). Be sure they will stand up to classroom use and that the child can make *music* with them. Make a sample and have a child try it. The author, with no special skills or tools, has made bamboo rhythm sticks, jingles, shakers, plastic trumpets, tom toms, and sand blocks for children's classes.

Easy instruments for the child to make with the help of the teacher
It is a good musical experience for a child to make and then play an instrument. It should be sturdy, make a good sound and be the right size for the child.

Be careful of decorations – the children may get carried away. Avoid things that will fall off when the instrument is played. Water paint comes off on hands or face. Use oil paint; or varnish on top of water paint. Glue lids on shakers firmly. Supervise carefully for safety.

Shakers – a few grains of rice, beans, pebbles in a plastic container with a lid. *Glue on the lid.*

Jingles — punch 5 holes in a leather strap, 5" long. Lace 3 small jingles into the middle 3 holes with a shoe lace. Tie the lace into a double knot through the other two holes. Leave 4" of lace at each end so the bells can be tied on wrists or ankles.

Rhythm sticks – cut half inch dowelling into 6"-9" lengths. Sand paper ends, then paint or varnish. Bamboo garden stakes make temporary rhythm sticks.

Drums – large plastic containers about 6" in diameter. Make a beater with dowelling. Use 2 litre plastic yogurt tubs. Discard lid. Turn upside down. A rounded hand, with curved fingers bouncing on the drum head, makes a good sound.

Trumpet — cut the top end off a large plastic bottle, the kind with a handle. Hold up to mouth and "toot" a well known tune. It stimulates uncertain singers to develop their vocal technique. Wash plastic bottle *well,* before making this instrument.

Further reading

Birkenshaw-Fleming, L.: **Come on Everybody, Let's Sing** Gordon V. Thompson Music, 1989

Bissell, Keith: **Singing and Playing for Primary Grades** Waterloo, 1977

Böhm, Suse: **Spiele mit dem Orff-Schulwerk** J.B. Metzlersche Stuttgart, 1975

Doloff, L.: **Das Schulwerk-Cognitive, Musical and Artistic Development** University of Toronto, 1993

Hall, Doreen: **Music for Children (A Teacher's Manual)** Schott & Sons, 1960

Keetman, Gunild: **Elementaria** Schott & Sons, 1974

Mandell and Wood: **Make Your Own Musical Instruments** Sterling, New York, 1959

Vermeulen, A.: **Chansons pour s'amuser, Songs to Play Games to Sing** Gordon V. Thompson Music, 1988

Vermeulen, A.: **Chansons pour s'amuser ... encore! More Songs To Play, Games To Sing** Gordon V. Thompson Music, A Division of Warner/Chappell Music Canada Ltd., Toronto, Canada, 1991

Student project

Make out an order form for basic percussion and tuned instruments for a co-op nursery school with an enrollment of 50 children. Each class of 12-15 children has a music period twice a week. The school has no instruments. The board of parents who run the school

(1) have assigned part of the annual budget for this purchase

or

(2) have limited funds, but several parents have volunteered to make instruments to supplement the purchased instruments.

   Mention prices, suppliers and other information along with the order form to be submitted to the board for final approval.

PART III
The Teacher

Contents of part three: the teacher

The teacher is the key

In this book, I have tried to give practical suggestions to the music specialist who wishes to teach young children and also to the early childhood specialist who wishes to have a music program in the school curriculum. In any educational situation, the teacher is the key. We have special challenges and responsibilities when our pupils are very young because the early years are critical in the learning process. We can open the door to the world of music, and our work can have a lasting effect on the life of each child we are privileged to teach.

The role of the early childhood teacher

To love little children is not enough.
We must have special qualities and abilities.
We must enjoy being with children and seeing them in action.

We cannot be effective teachers without extensive knowledge applied with understanding. The study of psychology, growth and development, mental and physical health, pedagogy and much supervised student practice are all included in early childhood teacher education. One student teacher remarked that she was amazed that "there was so much to it". Here are some of the roles we must play.

We must be ready to comfort the insecure or frightened child and be sure that each child is safe, when in our care
> – like a parent.

We must be happy with children's play and games
> – like a friend.

We must listen to and learn from the children
> – like a student.

We must observe, objectively, the children's general behaviour, affective responses, intellectual growth and skill development
> – like a researcher.

We must record and evaluate the child's learnings
> – like an educator.

We must be ready to intervene or redirect an activity with sensitive timing
> – like a director.

We must be ready and willing to invent an instrument, make a table or repair a hair-bow
> – like a creative handyman or woman.

Seemingly irrelevant questions or comments from the children must be dealt with clearly and honestly. "Teacher, why do you have gold in your teeth?"
> – like an unflappable dispenser of information.

We must have empathy with young children and their parents, and gain their trust and confidence
> – like a warm human being.

We must have a light touch and a special sense of humour. Take music seriously, but don't take yourself too seriously
> – like a good early childhood educator.

I hope this brief list will motivate the musician to seek further knowledge of early childhood education. Courses in class management and discipline, understanding behaviour and the learning process are necessary for the teacher.

Some of these subjects are included in a good parent education course. They would also be presented at workshops and conferences that are concerned with music and young children.

Another good way of learning about the young child is to work as a volunteer or a part time staff member in a well-run nursery school or day care centre. There you can observe the young child in action. I was a young piano teacher when I first stepped into a nursery school, many years ago – and I have never stepped out – for long.

Useful skills for the teacher

Movement skills

The teacher must be able to respond physically to music, to help the children experience music through movement. Preparing and teaching the movement games in this book will get you started. Try out and practise all game songs, no matter how simple they seem, *well before the class* with either imaginary children or a willing family.

You will have a better understanding of the relationship between movement and music, if you take classes in natural elementary movement, modern dance or folk dance, with a competent teacher. Also see information on page 200. Part II of this text, pages 34-37 have many suggestions for the beginnings of music and movement.

Be able to –
- Step, tap, pat or clap the even beat in all songs and games.
- Feel the beat "inside" without stepping, tapping etc. Start with a child's walking tempo (M.M. ♩ = 92–108)
- Keep an even beat at a faster (M.M. ♩ = 120) or slower (M.M. ♩ = 60) tempo.
- Know and model correctly and rhythmically the basic movements of children – walk, gallop, jump, rock, swing, run, hop and skip.
- Use room space with competence – sides, ends, centre, around, across, up and down.
- Develop strategy to teach children to move independently of others in their own space or place.
- Understand and show with movement – loud and soft, high and low, tempo, rhythm, the phrase and musical form.
- Clap, pat and step rhythm patterns with and without speech patterns. Include ♩, ♫, ♬, ♩ and 𝄽.
- Show meter with movement $\frac{2}{4}, \frac{6}{8}, \frac{3}{4}, \frac{4}{4}, \frac{5}{4}$.
- Know how to make a sitting circle, a standing circle, lines and rows with various ages and sizes of classes.
- Develop simple relaxation ideas. Use a quiet voice and a relaxed manner.
- Encourage, draw out and develop creative movement ideas with the children.
- Practice accompaniments for movement (see instrumental skills 179 & 181).
- Maintain controlled freedom in movement classes.

Speech skills

Speech is a stepping stone to singing. Through speech games, all the basic elements of music can be simplified and enjoyed by young children. All aspects of rhythm, dynamics, duration, pitch, timbre and form can be experienced through speech games. Combining body rhythms with speech patterns is a natural way for children to "do two things at once".
- Listen to your own voice. Practice natural speech with a tape recorder so you can hear how *you* sound. Your voice is a model to the children. Speak clearly and naturally, without silly childish mannerisms.

- Collect words, children's sayings and names of animals for rhythm patterns. Show real fruits, vegetables and flowers to add meaning to the activity. Children's names are often chanted in speech pattern games, but I feel empathy is needed here. Young children like to hear their names spoken in context – but stringing them into a rhythm pattern or repeating them 8 times loudly, softly, slowly, or quickly is *not* recommended.
- Learn at least 20-30 finger plays and children's rhymes. Bring out the music of the words. Exaggerate speech slightly, but do not pull the words out of shape.
- Listen and notate speech rhythms accurately: ma-ri-gold ♫ ♩ ; nee-dles and pins ♫♫ ♩. ♩ | ♩ gi-raffe.

About Talking

Early childhood teachers learn early in their training to "cut the verbal". To young children, "actions speak louder than words". They learn from experiences and activities, not from long verbal explanations. When I was a very new student teacher at the Institute of Child Study (University of Toronto) my first student practice was to help the three year old class with toilet routine. They were more familiar than I with the procedure, but I did manage to fasten up a button or two. I was struck dumb with terror, because I was being "casually observed" by the supervisor of the institute. When the last child had left, she came to me and said approvingly, "You are a natural". I was stunned. It did not occur to me until much later that I was being commended for *not* talking when no words were necessary.

Speak when necessary in a music class, but also use body language, gesture or demonstration. "Listen! The music will tell you what to do". At the Dalcroze Institute in Geneva, I heard a teaching master say to student teachers, "PARLEZ PEU!"

Singing skills

"I like music but I can't sing" is a common excuse for those who back away from singing. If you can *breathe* and have *vocal cords, you can sing;* but like any other muscles, they must be *used* to be *useful*. The song itself and the natural whole-hearted pleasure in singing it, are both more important for the children then a beautiful "trained" voice. I have taught many children to sing with my "kitchen voice". A few singing lessons to free your voice and help breathing and vocal techniques, will give you confidence to use your singing voice to teach music.

- The child's voice, on average, has a range of 5-6 notes and centres around F, so you do not need a large or high range to teach young children's songs or games.
- Learn to sing with no accompaniment; add simple accompaniments later.
- Learn to improvise with your voice. The pentatonic scale is easy and musical. Be aware of phrasing and form, i.e. improvise 2 bars in $\frac{2}{4}$ meter; $\frac{6}{8}$ meter. Improvise 4 bars in $\frac{2}{4}$ meter; $\frac{6}{8}$ meter, etc.
- A short singing conversation can be a creative experience for the young child.
- Chant spontaneous stories, rhymes or short dramas with puppets.

- Sing for movement games, keeping the tempo and beat. See list of traditional songs to accompany movement (page 181).
- Sing a song twice: first time loudly, 2nd time softly, keeping the *same* tempo.
- Sing a song softly *and* slowly (at the same time).
- Sing a song softly and quickly (at the same time).
- Know how to start a song at the correct pitch and be able to change the pitch if you wish to. Use a "pitched" instrument to help you – xylophone, tone bar, piano, pitch pipe.
- Gradually learn at least 100 songs with appropriate games or movement suitable for each age group.
- Make your own song book.
- Be able to clap the beat or step the beat while saying a rhyme or singing a song.
- Invent simple repetitive play motions for the children to feel the steady beat while they chant or sing.
- Sing in a choir to strengthen your voice and improve breathing skills. Sing rounds and canons with friends and colleagues to develop your sense of pitch.

Listening Skills

We must sharpen our ears to study or teach music. Moving, singing, playing an instrument and writing music involve careful listening. We must analyse what we hear. As you play listening games with the children, your own abilities will develop.
- Listen carefully to the children when they speak and sing. Tell the children that you are going to stop singing, so you can *listen* to them.
- Listen to the "sound environment" in your classroom. *Never* play records when the children are busy doing something else.
- Distinguish between rhythm patterns and beat. Tap the beat with your foot while you clap the rhythm pattern of a children's song.
- Identify the meter of children's songs and show your understanding in singing or playing. $\frac{2}{4}$ and $\frac{6}{8}$ are most common. $\frac{4}{4}$ and $\frac{3}{4}$ are less common.
- Know the shape of a melody. Does it go higher or lower or stay the same? Does it go in scale steps or larger steps?
- Sing pentatonic and major scales of C and D. See pages 187-188. Here is a challenge: Sing F pentatonic and major scales starting on middle C – Pentatonic s, 1, d r m s 1√ 1 s m r d, 1, s,

  Major   s, 1, t, d r m s 1√ 1 s f m r d t, 1, s,

  Take a breath at √

- Sing the key note and the starting note of a song. Get the pitch from a melody instrument. Sol-fa syllables will help you sing the correct pitch.
- Recognize and sing intervals that are in children's songs (see page 187)
  - major and minor 3rds
  - major 2nds
  - perfect 5ths and 4ths

- Young children's songs should not have 6th, 7th or octave leaps because many children cannot sing these intervals easily or correctly.
- Analyse each song so that you can recognize motives, phrases and form. This will help you remember a song. Study rhythm patterns and melody with care.
- Invent motives and phrases of rhythm and melody patterns. Use speech, singing and instruments. These are for echoing or question and answer games. Practice these before the class.
- A better ear for music can be developed through the study of Basic Musicianship. First the ability to listen and remember is practised, and then this leads to learning how to read and write music. A good early childhood music course should offer some Basic Musicianship.

Instrumental Skills

The teacher should be able to make music on one or more instruments and be able to use them as teaching tools for accompanying movement and percussion experiences. They are also useful for listening games and to play to the children for short music listening experiences.

Classroom Instruments – drum, woodblock, tambourine, etc.
- Practice all classroom instruments and play them *musically* so that you can produce a variety of sounds for movement accompaniment; use also for sound effects with rhymes and songs. Your instrumental technique should be a model for the children.
- Practice rhythms of basic movements of young children. Use a metronome (M.M. ♩ = 96) at first. (This is a common tempo for the clapping or walking of children).

  Walking ♩ ♩ ♩ ♩ – play with each metronome beat.

  Galloping ♩ ♪ ♩ ♪ ♩ ♪ ♪ – play so that accented sound (>) is with the metronome

  Running ♫ ♫ ♫ ♫ – play so that the accented sound (>) is with the metronome. It is twice as fast as walking; keep it steady and even.

  Skipping ♩ ♪ ♩ ♪ ♩ ♪ ♪ – like galloping (at this age level).

Try these rhythms on rhythm sticks, tambourine, bongo, wood block; A jingle bell stick or a maraca, tapped on the hand, gives a pleasing sound and is good for rhythm patterns.

- Practise 2 and 4 bar rhythm patterns using combinations of ♩, ♫, ♬, 𝅗𝅥 and 𝄽 on all these instruments e.g.

With speech

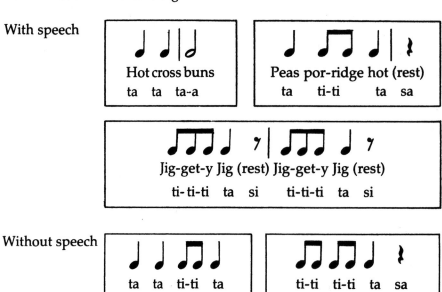

Without speech

Melody Instruments – Chime bars, xylophone, glockenspiel, metallophone.
- Practise mallet technique using both hands.
- Learn to play simple accompaniments(borduns) for children's songs.
- Play short introductions to songs. By doing so, you can clearly indicate to the children when to sing the first word.
- Find, play and sing the starting note of each song.
- Play *melodies* of all songs in this book, slowly at first, and then at a normal tempo. Be sure the rhythm is accurate.

The Soprano Recorder
- Take some private or class lessons, if you wish to use this beautiful little instrument. It is sturdy, inexpensive, easy to carry around and has no "tuning" problem. Play in a comfortable key.
- Play traditional melodies to accompany movement
    - Walk – The Muffin Man; Au clair de la lune
    - Gallop – The Farmer's in the Dell; Il était une bergère
    - Rock – Did you ever see a lassie; The Nightingale
    - Run – Oh Susanna; Yankee Doodle
    - Skip – Oats peas beans; En roulant ma Boule
- Improvise 8 or 16 bar melodies for these basic movements.
- Add melody when children are playing percussion instruments. This provides a framework for the experience.

- Play for listening and relaxation.

    May Song; Go Tell Aunt Rhody; Winter Goodbye

    Hush my Babe; Theme from Beethoven's 9th Symphony.

All above recorder melodies are found in Mario Duschene's **Method for the Recorder (Part 1)** Berandol Music Limited, Toronto, Ontario, 1957.

The Piano

(a) Pointers for pianists

- Adapt your pianistic skills. Use a light detached touch with little or no pedal. Emphasize the rhythm with a strong feeling for pulse and meter. Keep the melody going. Avoid very loud playing or a heavy left hand. Look at the children. Do *not* look at the keys or the music book. Be able to improvise for the basic movements of the child. Give variety, by using the whole piano and a range of tonalities. But play simply and clearly. Your "signals" from the piano must be clear and obvious to the class.

- Learn a repertoire of traditional melodies to accompany basic movements.

    Walk: $\frac{2}{4}$ or $\frac{4}{4}$ Baa, baa, black sheep; Au claire de la lune.

    Gallop: $\frac{6}{8}$ Ride a cock-horse; Savez-vous planter les choux?

    Floor rock: $\frac{3}{4}$ or $\frac{6}{8}$ Hush-a-bye, baby; I saw three ships come sailing in.

    Standing sway: $\frac{3}{4}$ or $\frac{6}{8}$ Hickory, dickory; London Bridge is broken down

    Run: $\frac{2}{4}$ Polly put the kettle on; Ladybird, Ladybird, fly away home.

    Skip: $\frac{6}{8}$ Girls and Boys come out to play; Here we go round the mulberry bush

    Jump: $\frac{4}{4}$ Polichinelle; Three blind mice

    These are all from: Oxford Nursery Song Book – Percy Buck O.U.P. (His piano arrangements are musical, very simple, and clear.)

- Learn to improvise in $\frac{2}{4}$, $\frac{3}{4}$, $\frac{5}{4}$ and $\frac{6}{8}$ meter.

(b) For those with limited skills on the piano.

- Take some piano lessons to gain technique.

- Memorize traditional melodies listed above. Simplify these by playing *melody only* in the right hand, and the first and lowest bass note of each bar with left hand.

    Rules for accompanists – Keep it steady, ignore wrong notes, and keep going!

- Learn to improvise 1. Take lessons in Keyboard Improvisation

    2. For easy chording and suggestions for accompanying, see **American Folk Songs For Children** (Doubleday) Ruth Seeger (pages 43-46)

General musicianship is more important than skill at the piano in early childhood music education.

The autoharp

This is an easy instrument to play, but does require some practice. It takes time and skill to *tune* the autoharp. The chords are found automatically, by pushing the correct letter button at the right moment. Strum on the strong first beat of every bar with a large felt pick. Begin with *one* chord songs, then proceed to two chord and then to *three* chord songs. Some help from an autoharp player who knows how to tune the autoharp and who can accompany children's songs in a quiet simple way, would help you. Use only with songs that you and the children know, and can sing the melody well.

One chord songs: (1) Ring around a rosy 101 (strum on the slash lines)

(2) Rain rain go away 165

Two chord songs: (1) The orchestra is playing, Tra la la la la la la . . . (159)

(2) Roll that big truck down to town, roll that big truck down to town . . . (143)

Three chord songs (1) I sent a letter to my love, And on the way I dropped it

A little doggie picked it up and put it in his pocket (117)

(2) hallowe'en is pumpkin time . . . . (requires F, C and G7 chords) 115
(Try it – your ear will tell you *which* chord and *when* to change)

Song books with autoharp chording indicated above the music
American Folk Songs for Children Ruth Crawford Seeger, Doubleday
Sally Go Round the Sun Edith Fowke, McClelland and Stewart

The children enjoy exploring the sounds of the autoharp. At first, they can strum *or* push the chord button, with the teacher helping with the other part.

Guide for reading, understanding and using the musical terms and symbols in this book

For those with little musical experience, this section describes briefly, some terms, signs and symbols found in this text. Have a pair of rhythm sticks, and an alto xylophone on hand for this section.

Note: Classes in Musicianship which combine reading, writing and singing are highly recommended. This subject is an integral part of the Dalcroze and the Kodaly approach to teacher education. Classes in musical theory will also be of help.

Rhythm terminology

1 Steady Beat or Regular Pulsation

This is the underlying element in music. It is like the tick-tock of a clock or the sound of marching feet. It is like your heart beat — find your heart beat and play it on your rhythm sticks.

2 Tempo (plural — Tempi) — the basic rate of speed. This is related to the child's motor skills. Here, a metronome will help you, e.g. — children's clapping 3 to 4 years ♩ = 60-80

4 to 5 years ♩ = 80-92

5 to 6 years ♩ = 92-112

So the teacher must be able to clap or play an even beat in this range of tempi. At the beginning, the teacher *follows* the natural tempo of the children and in time, the child will be able to follow different tempi. Never try to force young children to synchronize with an adult-set tempo, until they are ready.

3 Rhythm patterns

A series of long and short sounds as in the consecutive sounds of spoken language.

e.g. Hot Cross Buns

— — —

What is your name?

— — — —

4 Notation symbols

Note ♩, ♫ or ♩ — a measured sound

Rest 𝄽, 𝄾 — a measured silence

Duration — the length of time given to a note or a rest

They can be related to the basic movements of the child

Walking notes (Quarter notes) are written ♩ ♩ ♩ ♩ or a short form | | | |

Running notes (Eighth notes) are written ♫ ♫ ♫ ♫ or a short form ⊓ ⊓ ⊓ ⊓

— if there is only one ♪ or short form ⋀

Step Wait notes (Half notes) are written ♩ ♩ no short form

Swaying notes (Dotted Quarter notes) are written ♩. ♩. short form |. |.

5 Duration syllables

These are spoken in a rhythmical way and automatically give the correct rhythm

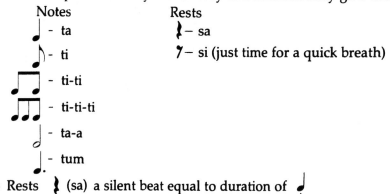

Notes

♩ - ta

♪ - ti

♫ - ti-ti

♬ - ti-ti-ti

𝅗𝅥 - ta-a

♩. - tum

Rests

𝄽 – sa

𝄾 – si (just time for a quick breath)

6 Rests

𝄽 (sa) a silent beat equal to duration of ♩

𝄾 (si) a silent beat equal to duration of ♪

Try saying and playing these on rhythm sticks. Then say and play the duration syllables of any song in this book.

Three of the songs in this text have slightly more difficult rhythm patterns. The words of the song will give you the correct rhythm.

Hop old squirrel p. 102

ti-ri-ti (eidel-dum)

Here sits a monkey p. 105

tim ri (sits a)

Here we go 'round the mountain p. 119

tri-o-la tim-ri (here we go 'round the)

Each teacher has a favoured version of these duration syllables. These are the ones I use and I have found them to be successful with young children.

Relating movement, symbol and duration syllables

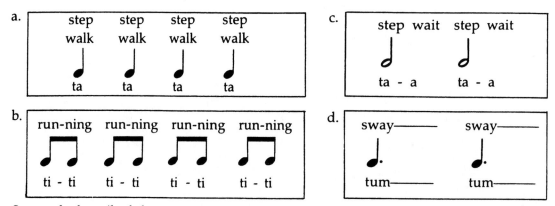

a.

step	step	step	step
walk	walk	walk	walk
♩	♩	♩	♩
ta	ta	ta	ta

b.

run-ning	run-ning	run-ning	run-ning
♫	♫	♫	♫
ti - ti	ti - ti	ti - ti	ti - ti

c.

step wait	step wait
𝅗𝅥	𝅗𝅥
ta - a	ta - a

d.

sway———	sway———
♩.	♩.
tum———	tum———

Say and play all of these examples on the drum, the rhythm sticks or on the piano as you improvise.

Relating words, movement, symbol and duration syllables

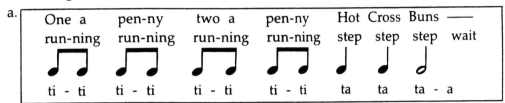

a.

One a	pen-ny	two a	pen-ny	Hot	Cross	Buns ——
run-ning	run-ning	run-ning	run-ning	step	step	step wait

ti - ti   ti - ti   ti - ti   ti - ti   ta   ta   ta - a

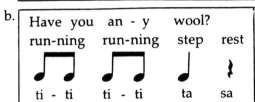

b.

Have you	an - y	wool?	
run-ning	run-ning	step	rest

ti - ti   ti - ti   ta   sa

Relating words, clapping, symbol and duration syllables

a.

Bought me a cat! The cat pleased me! [say and clap]

ta   ti - ti   ta si ti ta   ta   ta sa

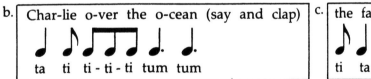

b.

Char-lie o-ver the o-cean (say and clap)

ta   ti   ti - ti - ti   tum   tum

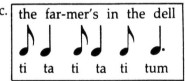

c.

the far-mer's in the dell

ti   ta   ti   ta   ti   tum

More rhythm terms

Meter — grouping of beats

Accent — emphasis on first beat of group. — is the sign

Bar lines — vertical lines to show groupings. They make music easier to read.

Bar (or *Measure*) — one group of beats

Time signature — indicates meter, the number of beats in each measure, and the duration of each beat

Rain   rain   go   a - way,

2 – number of beats
4 – duration of beat (♩)

ta   ta   ti - ti   ta

Many young children's songs are in this meter.

Here   we   go ga - ther - ing   nuts   in   May.

6 – number of beats
8 – duration of beat (♩.)

ti - ti - ti ti - ti - ti   ta   ti   tum

In $\frac{6}{8}$, there are two accented groups in each bar. This meter is very common in English rhymes and nursery songs.

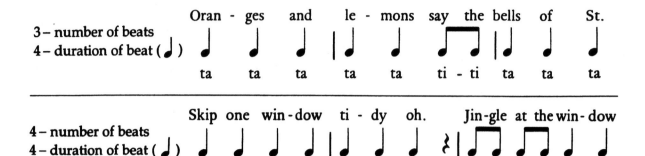

	Oran - ges	and	le - mons	say	the bells	of	St.
3 – number of beats							
4 – duration of beat (♩)							

ta   ta   ta   ta   ta   ti - ti   ta   ta   ta

	Skip one win-dow ti - dy oh.	Jin-gle at the win-dow
4 – number of beats		
4 – duration of beat (♩)		

ta   ta   ta   ta   ta   ta   ta   sa   ti - ti   ti - ti   ta   ta

Motif – A short musical idea (i.e. 2 bars)

Phrase – A longer musical idea (i.e. 4 bars)

Anacrusis – A "pick-up" sound, just before and leading to the accented beat.

Pitch notation

To associate the sound with the symbol, please use an alto xylophone with the absolute letter name on each wooden bar. A piano could also be used – find sounds with second finger. Music is written on a *staff* of 5 lines with 4 spaces in between the lines. They number from the bottom upwards.

The symbols for pitched sounds are called notes ♩ ♩ and are placed on these lines and spaces. These notes are named after the first seven letters of the alphabet A B C D E F G A B C D E F etc. These are *absolute* pitch names e.g. A always means the *sound* of A.

Ledger lines — are extra lines written below and above the staff for lower and higher sounding notes.

Treble Clef – a sign that curls around the *2nd* line of the staff is called the *G clef*, hence a note on the 2nd line is named G. If you write notes up and down alphabetically from G, using each successive line and space, and include the first ledger line below the staff, you will have written all the notes from middle C up to *high* F'(written F') F' means the sound on the 5th line of the treble staff. F means the first space on the treble clef. F, means the sound on the 4th line of the bass staff – those little ' or , are important.

G   F   E   D   middle C   G   A   B   C'   D'   E'   F'

Play and sing these with the alto xylophone. You are singing and playing by steps, like a ladder. Now, start on C and go up the ladder to F' and then down again. The space between each step is called an *interval* of a 2nd.

Interval — the distance between two sounds

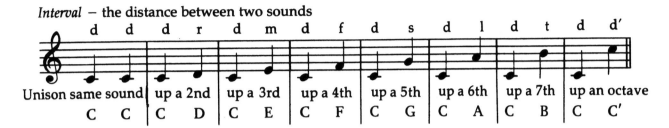

Unison same sound	up a 2nd	up a 3rd	up a 4th	up a 5th	up a 6th	up a 7th	up an octave
C C	C D	C E	C F	C G	C A	C B	C C′

Play and sing these with the alto xylophone

C C – same sound

C D – up a second

C E – up a third

– continue to C C′– up an octave

– try going down. C′B – down a second etc.

Melody – a series of sounds based on intervals. Children's songs move by steps and small intervals. Try to improvise melodies, using small steps or intervals on the xylophone.

Pentatonic scale – a 5 note scale. Melodies based on this scale usually move by small steps and intervals. Thus, many traditional children's songs are based on this scale e.g. Rain Rain; Bye Baby Bunting,; Teddy Bear etc. Remove [F] and [B] from the xylophone to make a C pentatonic scale and play these three songs "by ear", starting on G.

C Pentatonic scale

Sing and improvise melodies based on the pentatonic scale of C. Think of a four bar phrase; begin and end on either G or C.

Key note – C is the Key note in C *pentatonic* scale. C is the Key note in C *major* scale. Put the F and B back on the xylophone and play C major scale.

C Major scale

Change the Key note to D. To make it sound like a major scale, you must replace the F and C bars with F# and C#.

Sharp (#) – raises a sound half a step.

D Major scale   **Key signature**

D   E   F♯   G   A   B   C♯'   D'   Or   D   E   F♯   G   A   B   C♯'   D'

Key signature – written at the beginning of each line of music to tell the Key note. D major always has a Key signature with F# and C#. Play and sing D major scale up and down.

D Pentatonic scale

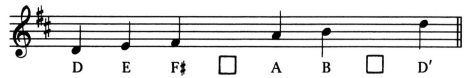

D   E   F♯   ☐   A   B   ☐   D'

There is no ⬚G and no ⬚C# in D pentatonic scale.

Play children's songs in D pentatonic "by ear". Rain Rain, Bye Baby and Teddy Bear will start on *A*, in this Key.

Sing and improvise melodies based on D pentatonic scale. Think of a 4 bar phrase; begin and end on A or D.

Transposition: Changing a song from one key to another i.e. C pentatonic to D pentatonic.

Relative Sol-fa Notation: This is a simple way to transpose from one key to another. It also facilitates reading and writing music. A music teacher of today needs to know this relative sol-fa system, as well as the absolute pitch system.

Relative Sol-fa Syllables

do– re– me– fa– so– la– ti– do

These are often shortened to

d– r– m– f– s– l– t– d

Scales written with Absolute *and* Relative System names

The *relative* system uses the same syllables for *every* key. It is called the *movable do* system. Using *absolute pitch* with sol-fa names is called the *"Fixed do"* system.

The Key of F – It has a key signature of B♭
Flat (♭) – lowers a sound a half step
Replace the B bar on the xylophone with B♭

Play and sing all C, D & F scales. Sing absolute pitch names first and then try relative sol-fa names as you play.

Improvise melodies based on C, D and F pentatonic scales. Sing absolute and relative names. Invent a rhythm pattern for your melody; e.g. ta ti-ti ta ta (I ⊓ I I)*

Now you are ready to *play* and *sing* all the songs in this book

1 Tap and say with duration syllables (ta, ti-ti)

2 Sing and play with absolute names (A, B, C)

3 Sing and play with relative "sol-fa" names (d, r, m)

4 Sing the words and play.

*Beethoven used this rhythm pattern repeatedly in the 2nd movement of the 7th symphony

Repeat signs

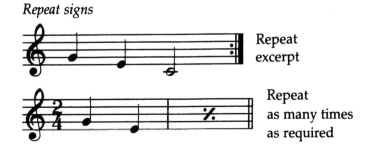

Repeat
excerpt

Repeat
as many times
as required

Fine (pronunciation: fee-nay) The end.

Organizing and Planning Music Experiences

As music teachers, we must plan our work with care, so that we can make the best use of the time we have with the children.

Goals and Objectives

There should be definite goals in a teaching plan. To be sure, there are a number of different methods to achieve these goals. My method is to start with an element of music e.g. "tempo" and introduce it to young children in a way that they can understand. I draw attention to "tempo" through "play", or a game. Then the children are encouraged to imitate and feel the element themselves. And then, perhaps on another day, we suggest that this element be used in a different game, in a more creative way.

Random musical activities that entertain, rather than educate, do not challenge the child's interest or capacity for long, and can become dull and boring. Therefore, I plan with a musical goal in mind; then, I choose the game or song to illustrate it.

If some real progress is achieved at every lesson, the children look forward eagerly to each succeeding lesson.

The following elements of music are listed separately to help in the lesson planning. The easiest element for children to understand is "dynamics". This is a "teacher's word" of course — the children call it "loud" and "soft".

Dynamics — degrees of sound.
loud (f) and soft (p)
1 Draw attention to the concept, so that children will become aware. "I will play loud sounds on the drum. Listen! Now I will play soft sounds on the drum".
2 Children imitate
Clap your hands with me — loudly, then softly. Change when I change from loud to soft.
3 Use in a different activity, creatively.
What animal has a loud voice? Be that animal.
What animal has a soft voice? Be that animal.
Use wide contrasts with beginners. When they are ready, add
- medium sounds (mf or mp)
- same sounds e.g. all soft
- getting louder (crescendo $<$)
- getting softer (diminuendo $>$)
- a sudden loud sound (accent $>$)

Rhythm — the flow of music.
Even pulsation — feeling the beat
1 Draw attention with a real clock that "ticks". This clock says "Tick-Tock-Tick-Tock".
2 Imitates — play your rhythm sticks with me and say "Tick-Tock-Tick-Tock".
3 Another activity — Be in a parade. What will you be? How does the band walk — show me.

The above teaching sequences build concepts of music. The following elements can be sequenced in a similar manner.

Tempo
1 Fast and slow
2 Moderate
3 Getting slower
4 Getting faster (difficult for young children to control)
Rhythm Patterns
1 A mixture of long and short sounds
2 Ostinato is a short rhythm pattern, repeated throughout song.
Rests
𝄽 and 𝄾 Beats of silence
Dividing the beat

| | | |

⊓ ⊓ ⊓ ⊓

Meter and Accent

1̄ 2 3; 1̄ 2 3 4; 1̄ 2 3 4 5 ; 1̄ 2.

1̄ 2 3 4̄ 5 6

Pitch
1 High and low sounds
2 The same sound
3 High, middle and low sounds
Melody
Sounds going higher, sounds going lower or staying the same.

Timbre
The quality of the sound — everybody's voice *sounds* different; different kinds of animals and instruments *sound* different.

Form
Phrase feeling. Note which phrases are different and which are the same in a song. Show this with a rhythmic action
— echo phrases (both are the same)
— question and answer phrases (each is different)
Music Design
A; AB; ABA; ABACA (this is a Rondo); ABCDABCD — (Canon or Round)
                    ABCDABCD

What skills must we teach to attain our musical goals and to enrich musical experiences?

This is my general list in a suggested pedagogical order. My expectations would vary with the age, the maturity of the children, and also equipment available and teaching environment. The following list starts at age 3 and develops to ages 6-7.

- Paying attention and listening
- Moving with music · Starting · Stopping
- Learning to sing
- Developing technique with instruments
- Rhythmic sureness, co-ordination and control
- Echoing rhythm and melody patterns
- Developing musical memory
- Moving and Singing − doing *two* things at once
- Moving and Singing and Playing instruments − doing *three* things at once
- Clapping or playing rhythmic ostinati
- Singing "question and answer" phrases
- Improvising (creating) with movement, speech, melody and instruments
- Saying rhythm syllables − ta ti-ti ta-a; ti-ti ta ti-ti ta etc.
- Reading rhythm symbols − ♩, ♫, ♩, ⁊
- Writing rhythm symbols − ♩, ♫, ♩, ⁊
- Sing melodies with hand levels
- Developing inner hearing

Student project
Note the level of the musical skills in your class. How long will you be working with these children? Make a sequenced plan of the skills you would teach, in the above time frame, to attain your musical goals.

Guide for observing individual children in the music class

1 *Musical Learning*

Does child show evidence of developing these skills? Give examples.

2 *Physical Behavior*

Ability to walk, run, gallop, skip, step wait, turn, etc.

Ability to manipulate ball, ribbons, scarves, etc.

Note instrumental technique – is child learning to make a good sound?

Accurate and rhythmical response in finger plays, action songs, and singing games.

Identify parts of body, note dominant side (left or right).

Show loud/soft, fast/slow, high/low, *through movement.*

Ability to relax and listen quietly.

3 *Language*

Does child make spontaneous comments and ask questions?

Does child use single words or sentences?

Note any words or sounds child has difficulty in pronouncing.

Can child follow oral directions?

Any problems with speech or hearing?

4 *Cognitive Behavior*

Can child remember names of children? instruments? games?

Can child remember words of rhymes? fingerplays? songs?

Can child remember melodies of songs?

Can child recognize melodies of songs, if "la-la-la" is substituted for words?

Can child identify and perform loud/soft, fast/slow, high/low?

5 *Emotional Behavior*

Does child move, sing, play instruments and games with confidence?

Does child persevere when not successful the first time?

Does child show anger, fear, hostility, timidity, crying, tension?

Is child friendly to children and adults? protective? sympathetic? helpful?

Is child easily distracted? Short attention span?

6 *Social Behavior*

Is child happy in group activities – as a leader or a follower?

Can child wait for a turn and co-operate, usually?

Does child help tidy equipment "when it is time?"

Does child stay on "outskirts" of activities?

Last but *not* least:

7 Imagination, creativity, contributing ideas and suggestions? Improvising in movement, with speech or song, with instruments?

Student project

Select a child to observe, and write a behaviour study, using this guide.

Planning for music time

Before planning individual classes, we should prepare a master plan for an entire series of classes. Games with movement, speech, singing and instruments are linked to the teaching of musical goals and skills. Themes such as special holidays (i.e. Hallowe'en) are included in the plan.

Much time is given to review and repetition of games and songs. This is an excellent way to develop and practise singing skills. Children love games, and are never bored with the repetition of a favorite one.

Selecting materials

1 Use material of good musical quality for movement, games, speech, singing, instruments and listening. We are responsible for influencing the musical taste of the children.

2 Select traditional folk songs and good composed music with rhythmic vitality.

3 Songs for children to sing should match their aural and physical (vocal cords, lungs) development. At the beginning, songs based on the pentatonic scale with a range of about 6 notes, fit this criteria. The words are important to the children, and should fit the melody, exactly.

4 Music for *listening* could have a larger vocal and language range and be based on major and minor scales or other modes.

5 Children will learn about music, if they enjoy their musical experiences.

A plan for one class

I believe that there should be a definite plan for each class and that it should be *written* in a note book for future reference. The musical needs of the child must be considered and the musical materials chosen with care. The plan should be flexible so that a child's spontaneous idea or interest, can easily be incorporated into the activities. Once a child brought a snail in a jar to the class. Its "horns", the way it moves, what it eats and its shell were all included in a happy musical game at the beginning of the class.

> Snail, snail, put out your horns,
> I'll give you bread and barley corns.

How to teach a new song

1 Prepare well before the class with accompanying game or rhythmical action. A clear picture or a small object may clarify new ideas and stimulate interest.

2 The first time, the teacher sings the whole song simply and musically, at its natural speed. Start on the *correct note* and sing with *good pitch*. Sing the words clearly and naturally. Repeat short songs several times, encouraging the children to join you.

3 Feel the rhythmic pulse of the song, as you show the actions.

4 Sit at the same level as the children, *so that good eye contact is possible*. Use no instrumental accompaniment, at first.

5 Praise and encourage the children's first efforts. Gently correct words, melody or difficult phrases. Allow time, and several sessions, for the children to learn a song.

6 Can the children sing the song when you stop and listen? Can a child sing it alone?

Suggested plan for 10 music-time classes

Setting: Day Care Centre, Nursery School – large music room – 20 children, 3-4 years – one adult helper; Classes are twice a week and about 20 minutes in length.

September	Theme	Goal, Skill, Instruments	Musical Material
Class 1	Getting Acquainted	Teacher's Name Children's Names Maracas; Bells	Rhyme: Open Them 72 Game: Point to The Ceiling 131 Song: Clap Clap Clap Your Hands (l s m) 93
Class 2	Playground Fun	Start. Stop. Walk. Gallop. Space. Follow in a Group	Clap/Stop with my Drum 38 Walk/Stop with my Drum 38 Song: Clap. Pat. Walk with Me 93
Class 3	Day Time Night Time	Loud. Soft. Floor Games Small Hand Drums	Rhyme: Clap Your Hands (loud/soft) 93 Space Games 36 Song: Bye-o, Baby 9
Class 4	Horses, Ponies Review	Even Beat Horses Walk-Say "Clip Clop" Rhythm Sticks	Rhyme: Shoe the Old Horse 9 Game: See the Ponies 125 Play and Say *Clip Clop*, Play, Say, Walk 155
Class 5	Clocks	Faster. Slower Beat. Wood Block Review: Even Beat	Rhyme: Hickory Dickory Dock 73 Song: Tick Tock Says the Clock 162 Be a Clock, Be a Mouse
Class 6	Rain	Loudly. Softly. Push Away Rain, on the *Beat* Bells. Sticks. Drums	Song: Rain Rain Go Away 92 Poem: The Rain Is Raining 165 The Orchestra Is Playing 159
Class 7 *See next page.	Farm Animals	Making Sounds Moo Like a: Cow, Pig, Duck, Horse Jingle Bells	Finger play: This Little Pig 72 Song: Bell Horses 94 Space Games With Animals – Animal Walks 37
Class 8	Cats, Kittens Review	Quickly. Slowly. Walk like a cat and *Meow* Run like a Kitten and *Meow*	Game: The Old Grey Cat 107 Rhyme: Finger Play Song – I Love Little Pussy 116 Rhyme: ABC, Tumble Down 85
Class 9	Dogs, Puppies	Soft. Loud. *Barking* Move like Dogs Instruments	Rhyme: Bow Wow Wow 84 Game: I Sent A Letter 117 Play and Sing: I Sent A Letter 117
Class 10	Bears	Teddy Bear Rhythm (♫ ♩) Low, Middle, High Voice	Game: Teddy Bear, Turn Around 98 Story: The Three Bears 135 Dance: Fuzzy Wuzzy 106

Continue with your own plan, offering a variety of happy musical experiences to the class in a developmental sequence.

A plan for one class

This is class number 7 on the Master Plan for the same group of children in the same setting.
    Theme: Farm animals   Musical Goal: Different sounds
    Prepare: Clear pictures of Cow, Pig, Duck, Pony and other farm animals; a bell for each child.

Introduction
– Children come into music room: *welcome,* and *hello,* to all
– Let's go walking all around the farm – come with me
    Teacher walks and sings *"The farmer's in the dell"* **121**

Move
Gallop like a pony (lesson 4)
– *stop* when I say "Whooah"
– *go* when I say "giddy-up"
– sit and rest for a minute, the ponies are tired
– what other animals would you like to be? Show pictures of Cow, Pig, Duck and others.
– *be* a cow (Pig, Duck etc). Make a sound like a cow. The drum will tell you when to start and when to stop. Play and say Moo-oo to accompany the cows. (Oink, Quack etc.)

Speech
Sit near me – hold out your hands.
– Each of your fingers is a little pig. Say *"This little pig"* **72**
– now play it with your other hand.

New song with instruments
Bell Horses **94**
– stand and sing, tapping bells on the beat
– gallop with bells, *while teacher sings song* (most children cannot sing *and* gallop.)
– repeat several times, then put bells back in their box

Review
Rain, Rain **92**
– finger play
– motion on the beat (lesson 6)

Memory
Who can sing "Bell Horses, Bell Horses"? (first line only)

Relaxation
Teacher sings "everything's sleeping (4 verses cow, pig, duck and pony) **51**
Goodbye – when I sing "goodbye, Mark" – go back to your play room.
"Good-bye", singing each child's name to *s s m*

Suggested plan for 8 music classes in the 2nd term

Setting: Music School – large bare room 30′ × 40′ – 12 children, 4-5 years old;
Music classes are one hour long, once a week.

January	Theme	Musical Goal, Skill	Musical Material
Class 9	What did you do on your holiday?	Question and Answer 85, 86 Improvise 143 Review Winter Songs	Rhythm: Pussy Cat Where Have You Been? 85 Rhyme: Hello, Hello, Hello Sir 87 Game: Who Has the Penny? 141
Class 10	Winter	Review Meter Technique on Timpani 160	Winter Games 56 Rum Tum 160 Game: Down Came A Lady 118
Class 11	Ice	Feeling and Moving to $\frac{3}{4}$ Meter Feel and Show the *Rest*	Skating With a Twirl 54 Rhyme: Pease Porridge Hot 83 Song: I Love Little Pussy 116
Class 12	Animals that like the snow	Rhythm patterns. Sounds Animal Names – Clap 77 Play Animal Name on Percussion	Names 76 Rhyme: Hello, Sir (Review) Game: The Farmer's in the Barn 132

February			
Class 13	Friends	Echo Games 76 Voice Recognition 114	Walk/Stop With a Friend 48 Partner Games 53 Game: The Big Ship 49
Class 14 See next page	Valentine	Partner Walks Beat/Rhythm Patterns Rhythm Sticks. Hand Drums	Game: Ring Around 101 Rhyme: Roses Are Red 76 Play and Sing: Beat/Rhythm
Class 15	Review	Melody Echo 139, 140 Song Recognition 142	I Like Spring 139 Children's Choice (Make a list.)
Class 16	Open Classes for Parents	Move. Sing. Listen. Play	Children's list of songs and games.

Continue with your own plan, offering a variety of happy musical experiences to the class, in a developmental sequence.

Suggested plan for one class

This is class number 14 on the Master Plan for the same group of children (4-5 years).
   Theme: Valentine   Musical Goal: Beat. Rhythm Patterns.
   Prepare: 6 pairs of rhythm sticks; 6 hand drums; one real rose (if possible); 12 squares of thin coloured fabric (24 X 24 inches).

Move:
Opening: Greet each child
– Free play with squares (4-5 minutes) **65**
– Listening Game – *Skip* by yourself; *walk* with a partner, stepping on the beat. (Children follow *walk* or *skip* cue from teacher's instrument.) **53**
Partner Games **53**
– Clap: 1, 2, 3,
         you and me
– Pat a cake – with partner (on Beat) **53**
– Ring around a rosy (3 verses) **101**

Speech:
Roses are red **76**
– say and clap *beat*.
– say and clap rhythm pattern
– say and clap "Valentine"   What other valentine words can you clap? **82**

Singing games:
Down came a lady (try to step on the beat. Lift your knees a little) **118**
Who's that knocking? tapping? **114**

Memory:
"Who can remember the song about the King?" (verse 2 of "Ring around") **101**
" – Who can remember the song about the robin?" (verse 3 of "Ring around")

Individual:
A child walks like the King's daughter around the circle. "How would she carry a pail of water? **101**
"We will find the beat of your walk and clap it." Ask another child.

Instruments:
"When I say your name, come and get a pair of sticks **or** a hand drum – You choose the sound you want to play." **157, 158**
– Sing and play rhythm pattern of "Who's that".

" – Play this *rhythm* pattern while I play the *beat* on the triangle"
" – Play the *beat* while I play the *rhythm* pattern on the triangle"

Relaxation:
"Go for a skip; when the music changes to "resting" lie down for a rest." **41, 51**

Goodbye:
"When I say your name, find a partner, and walk out together, stepping on the beat." **53**

Footnote to planning

Begin and end a class with a favorite well-known song or game. It gives the children a comfortable feeling of order and security.

Focus on one ability or element of music during each lesson, through movement, singing and instrumental games. This gives the children several opportunities to practise the skill or to understand the element. For example, if a child is not able to skip (many 4 year olds cannot), this rhythm pattern ♩ ♫ ♫ ♫ ♪ will come up again in the same lesson with instruments, or in a song.

Evaluation

Did the children enjoy the class?
Did each child participate?
What should be repeated or reviewed?
Did I achieve my musical goal?

Student project

1 On *one* page, prepare a general plan for a unit of 10 consecutive "music times" for the coming term. State ages of the children, the number in the group and the time span of each music period. Is it a daily, bi-weekly or weekly experience? Briefly describe the setting – Nursery School, Day Care centre or Music Studio. Have the plan apply to your teaching situation, if possible.

2 On *one* page, prepare a detailed plan for the 5th class of the unit.

Further reading

Allin, N., Birkenshaw, L., Queen, L.: **Music Is Special Children Are Special** Ministry of Education (Ontario), 1981

Almy, Millie: **The Early Childhood Educator At Work** McGraw Hill, 1975

Andress, B. and others: **Music In Early Childhood** MENC, 1973

Andress, B.: **Music Experiences In Early Childhood** Holt Rinehart Winston, 1980

Aronoff, F.: **Music and Young Children** Holt Rinehart Winston, 1980

Ben-Tovim and Boyd: **The Right Instrument For Your Child** Gollancz, 1985

Birkenshaw-Fleming, L.: **Music For All: Teaching Music for People With Special Needs** Gordon V. Thompson Music, 1993

Carter, P. and Landis, B.: **The Eclectic Curriculum In American Music Education** MENC, 1973

Forrai, K. (trans. Sinor, J.): **Music in Preschool (Revised Edition)** Corvina, 1994

Hall, D., Editor: **Orff-Schulwerk in Canada** Schott, 1992

Ingram, Jay: **Talk Talk Talk** Viking, 1992

Kazdan, R.: **A Parent's Guide To Successful Piano Lessons** Palmerston Press (Toronto), 1991

McKay, Donald K.: **Creative Teaching In Early Childhood Education–2nd ed.** Harcourt, Brace and Jovanivitch Canada, 1993

Palmer, M. and Sims, W.: **Music In Pre-Kindergarten** MENC, 1993

Wilson, Frank: **Tone Deaf and All Thumbs** Random House, 1987

Zemke, Sr. Lorna: **Music For the Unborn Child** Silver Lake College, Manitowoc, W1, U.S.A. 1988

Information for teachers

Teacher's associations with information about early childhood music education (courses, conferences, professional development):

1 **Advanced Certificate in Early Childhood Music Education**

This certificate program was developed between the Ryerson University Continuing Education Division, the School of Early Childhood Education, and the Royal Conservatory of Music. It is designed specifically for educators and musicians who work with young children.

Ryerson University Continuing Education
350 Victoria Street
Toronto, Ontario M5B 2K3

2 **Association For Early Childhood Education (Ontario)**
40 Orchard View Blvd., Suite 211
Toronto, Ontario M4R 1B9

3 **Dalcroze Society of Canada**
17 Washington Avenue
Toronto, Ontario M5S 1L1

4 **Early Childhood Music Association of Ontario (ECMA of 0)**
Royal Conservatory of Music
273 Bloor St. West
Toronto, Ontario M5S 1W2

5 **Early Childhood Diversity Network Canada (ECDNC)**
Welcome House Nursery
132 St. Patrick Street
Toronto, Ontario M5T 1V1

6 **International Society of Music Education (ISME)**
Early Childhood Commission
ISME International Office
University of Reading, Bulmershe Court
Reading RG6 1HY United Kingdom

7 **Music For Children (Musique pour enfants)**
Faculty of Music
University of Toronto
Toronto, Ontario M5S 1A1

Some commercial resources for early childhood music, books, instruments

Empire Music Co. Ltd.
8553 Main Street
Vancouver, B.C. V5X 3M3
Tel (604) 324-7732
Toll-Free 1-800-663-5979

Long & McQuade Ltd.
1744 Midland Avenue
Scarborough, Ontario M1P 3C2
Tel (416) 751-9709
Toll-Free 1-800-268-6525

The Sound Post
130 Harbord Street
Toronto, Ontario M5S 1G8
Tel (416) 323-1839
Toll-Free 1-800-363-1512

Waterloo Music
3 Regina St. North
Waterloo, Ontario N2J 4A5
Tel (519) 886-4990
Toll-Free 1-800-563-9683

Conclusion

"What do I need to know to offer genuine musical experiences to young children?"

In this book, I have tried to give you some of the answers from my own experience. It has taken many years to reach this stage, but it has been an exciting and fulfilling journey – and one which never ends. Every time I enter the child's world of music, I learn something about children and something about music. There are two disciplines to answer to – *Early Childhood Education and Music Education* – which are developmentally appropriate for young children.

Some of the skills and abilities for teachers that I have listed in Part III, may be achieved with a little thought and planning. Others are a challenge, and will require study and practice.

Do what you *can*, now, and gradually add techniques, teaching skills and musical repertoire. Music is a subject to be savoured slowly. Enjoy it as you learn. Then you can pass this enjoyment on to the children.

General Index

Index of Movement Games

Alphabetical Index of First Lines of Speech Games and Rhymes

Alphabetical Index of
First Lines of Songs and Games

Alphabetical Index of Sound and Listening Games

Index of Instrument Games

Addenda

Since 1953, ISME, the International Society of Music Education, has brought together music educators from around the world who are committed to excellence in Music Education.

Addenda 1

The 16th ISME Conference was held in Eugene, Oregon, in July, 1984, where the theme "Music for a Small Planet" was proclaimed. My presentation was entitled "Music and Music Education As Vehicles For Intercultural Cooperation and Global Understanding".

Addenda 2

The Early Childhood Commission of the 18th ISME Conference was held in Brisbane, Australia in 1988. My topic was "Early Childhood Development And Musical Experiences". This paper was reprinted in a number of music education journals and also has been documented in the Library of the J.W. Goethe Universitat in Mainz, Germany.

Addenda 1

Music and Music Education As Vehicles For
Intercultural Cooperation And Global Understanding

How can a music teacher of very young children promote the noble and vital goals of intercultural cooperation and global understanding? – the goals of all men and women of peace, who are living on this small and troubled planet. I believe that music education can promote social skills and attitudes in the developing child which, in turn, can promote the ideals of worldwide understanding and cooperation.

The early childhood educator believes that human beings become the way they are because of the way they were molded as young children. Early experiences have a strong effect on the development of attitudes and the personality of the young child. Each child is an individual with strengths and weaknesses – with likes and dislikes. Despite these very human traits, children can learn to accept themselves as they are, and at the same time, learn to accept and be comfortable with other individuals.

In the home, at school, and in the community, these are first steps toward maturity and being at home in the world at large. In teaching objectives and activity planning, the early childhood educator tries to achieve a healthy balance among the interrelated areas of growth and development – physical, emotional, intellectual and social. They try to stimulate the creative instinct and the child's capacity for wonder, joy and playfulness.

I believe that the early childhood *music* education teacher must have similar objectives. We must consider individual differences and the development of the whole personality of the child in planning musical curriculum and activities. How can early music education affect the growth, the development and the maturation of young children? Music is like the sun – its ray can touch all areas of human development.

- Music can stimulate physical development – music and movement activities, finger plays and traditional singing games, teach coordination, cooperation and relaxation.
- Music can stimulate emotional development – "role-playing" games, songs and small improvised musical dramas can vent emotional feelings and foster self-control and self-discipline.
- Music can stimulate intellectual development – all the rhythmic and melodic elements of music invite recognition, comparison and classification.
- And, in the developmental area that we are addressing this afternoon, the music class can stimulate social development – learning to be an individual in a group and to be a leader or a follower, learning to participate with joy and confidence, learning self-control and sharing with others – all of these lead to social maturity. Furthermore, social experiences in the music class promote communication, sympathetic understanding and healthy relationships with other human beings. These are foundations for the development of intercultural and global understanding, the theme of this international music education conference.

Now, let us have some musical experiences that could influence social development. I offer five musical examples – I ask you to participate in these traditional games selected from several cultures. There is a remarkable similarity in the early childhood games of every culture. The baby shows interest in the human face from birth, and by three months, there is social interaction between the baby and those close by. Infants thrive on the warmth of individual attention. This social interaction can be heightened by the music of traditional lullabies, dandling rhymes and finger and foot plays. Babies respond to these happy games with pre-verbal musical sounds and babbling, stimulating language development and social communication.

Here is an English hand patting game that could be played with a very young **baby**. [Demonstrate] Now try it with the person sitting beside you. Decide who will be the baby and who will be the adult.

Baby Game

Pat a cake   ba - ker's man,   Bake a   cake as   fast you can.

Two-year-olds are interested in other children but are not yet ready to share toys or play cooperatively. However, a teacher or parent can initiate short experiences of music-making with individual children or small groups, using nursery rhymes, singing chants and finger games. The child has the option of joining in or observing these early musical and social activities. We wait until the child is ready to join and participate in the group.

Here is a peeking game to play with a 2-year-old:

Baby Game

Peek a   boo,   I   see you,   Peek a   boo,   yes I   do.

Three-year-olds are increasingly interested in social play with other children. They enjoy short group experiences with an adult who can lead and join in the fun of clapping, singing and dancing games. Threes are beginning to experience the joy of conversation and communication. Musical rhymes, poetry and game songs can stimulate this speech and this interaction between a child and an adult. This English rhyme game is often played on a young child's toes. But it can also be played on the fingers.

> This little pig went to market
> This little pig stayed home
> This little pig had roast beef
> This little pig had none
> This little pig says "wee wee wee wee" all the way home.

Four-year-olds are eager to learn about their immediate environment and the people in it. They ask many questions about what they see around them, but they are also curious and full of questions about the larger world of which they are becoming aware. But because they are growing and learning at a rapid rate, there are often problems. Sometimes four-year-olds are co-operative and considerate of others, but at other times they are negative and selfish. However, the appropriate musical activity can have a therapeutic effect and can help them enjoy social activities with their friends.

I learned the next finger play from a 4-year-old boy in Sapporo, Japan. His mother wrote down the music and the phonetic syllables for me. This afternoon, it will be a *multicultural* song. It does not follow the usual numerical or melodic sequence. It will be easier for me to demonstrate:

- first in English
- now in French
- now in Japanese
- now in your language

Five Finger Game   i = ee   Japan

Ich   Ni   San   𝄽   Ni   no Shi   no   Go   𝄽
1   2   3   2   & 4   &   5

San   Ich   Ni   no Shi   no   Ni   no Shi   no   Go   𝄽
3   1   2   & 4   &   2   & 4   &   5

The five-year-old is interested in *people*, what they are doing and where they are going. Social relationships are important to them, and they are ready to play and learn in a group, that is, if social needs have been met in the earlier years. When children hold hands in a traditional singing game, they are proclaiming the democracy of the circle formation and the social joys of singing together. Five-year-olds are eager to look at picture books and listen to stories about science, space discoveries and the wonders of the world, and beyond. Many have now ventured into the wider world of school and travel, where they can test the social skills learned in earlier years.

Now join me in a game that I learned from a teacher in Jamaica. She played it this way as a child. [Demonstrate] Stand up. Face your partner:

Clapping Game   Caribbean

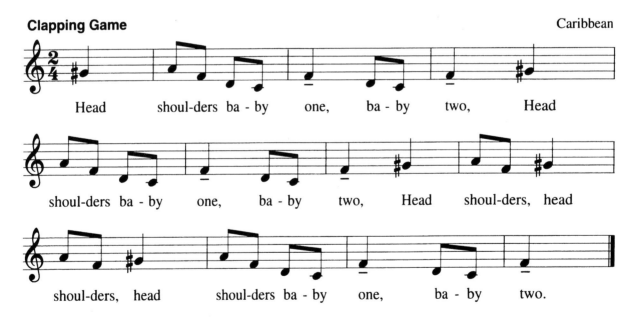

Head   shoul-ders ba - by   one,   ba - by   two,   Head

shoul-ders ba - by   one,   ba - by   two,   Head   shoul-ders, head

shoul-ders,   head   shoul-ders ba - by   one,   ba - by   two.

In this brief chronology, we have touched on the ages and stages of the young child and how musical activities can influence the socialization process. Children learn much from each other, especially in a happy group environment.

The music education philosophies and methodologies of Jaques-Dalcroze, Zoltan Kodaly and Carl Orff strongly endorse a group play environment for early musical learning. Moreover, these three great teachers of the twentieth century showed remarkable insight into the total development of the personality and the importance of early learning, in their pedagogy and in their writings.

Jaques-Dalcroze has written: "The earlier we instil tastes and convictions in a man, the more sure we may be of their durability and solidity. We should regard the child as the man of tomorrow."

Emile Jaques-Dalcroze (1865-1950)
Rhythm Music and Education,
First published in 1921

Zoltan Kodaly says: "The years between three and seven are educationally much more important than the later ones. What is spoiled or omitted at this age cannot be put right later on. In these years, man's future is decided practically for his whole lifetime."

Zoltan Kodaly (1882-1967)
Music in the Kindergarten, Lecture, 1940

Carl Orff proclaims: "To awaken those forces which shape the personalities of our very young, is a goal worth every effort."

Carl Orff (1895-1982)
Music for Children, American Edition 2

Soon, our young children will be venturing into the twenty-first century. Have we introduced music to them in such a way that it will still be an important part of their lives? And do our teacher training courses in *early childhood education*, and in *music education*, encourage research and practical study into the best beginnings of musical learning? And do these courses acknowledge the socializing influence of the arts? Are music and art considered to be as important as any other area in the early childhood curriculum?

Many young children in Canada attend preparatory music classes for infants, toddlers, three-, four- and five-year-olds. Our multicultural society is reflected in these classes, as it is in the music programs offered in the growing number of day care centres, nursery schools and also in the public school educational systems. Though the way is not always smooth, cultural diversity is cultivated along with national unity in our unique "Canadian way". I have observed early childhood music classes across our country from Victoria on the Pacific coast to Halifax on the Atlantic coast. I have noted how music teachers strive to instill in these young children a respect for individual and cultural differences. Surely this will lead, in some small way, to our hope for the twenty-first century – intercultural cooperation and global understanding.

References

Almy, Minnie: **The Early Childhood Educator at Work** McGraw Hill, 1975

Böhm, Suse: **Spiele mit dem Orff-Schulwerk** J.B. Metzlersche, Stuttgart, 1975

Bruner, J.: **Toward a Theory of Instruction** Harvard University Press, 1971

Forrai, Katalin: **The Influence of Music on the Development of Three-Year-Old Children** Kodaly Seminar in Kecskemét, 1970

LaPierre, Laurier et al.: **To Herald a Child (Nos Enfants)** Canadian Journal of Early Childhood Education, April 1982

McLeod, Keith A., editor: **Multicultural Early Childhood Education** Faculty of Education, University of Toronto, 1984

Montessori, Maria: **Education for Human Development** Schocken Books, New York, 1976

Moog, H.: **The Musical Experiences of the Young Child** Trans. Clarke, Scott, 1976

Piaget, J. and Inhelder: **The Psychology of the Child** Basic Books, New York, 1969

Seeger, Ruth Crawford: **American Folk Songs for Children** Doubleday, U.S.A., 1948

Simons, G.: **Early Childhood Musical Development, Research Abstracts** MENC, Reston, Virginia, 1978

Stone, J. and Church, J.: **Childhood and Adolescence – The Psychology of the Growing Person** Random House, New York, 1957

Wood, Donna: **Move, Sing, Listen, Play** Gordon V. Thompson Ltd., Toronto, Canada, 1982 Revised edition 1995 by Gordon V. Thompson Music, A Division of Warner/Chappell Music Canada Ltd., Toronto, Canada

Addenda 2

Early Childhood Development And Musical Experiences

What was your earliest musical experience?
What was your unhappiest musical experience?
What was your happiest musical experience?

These three questions were asked at the first lecture of two different Early Childhood Music Education courses given in Toronto, Canada in 1986. One course was offered by the Ryerson School of Early Childhood Education and the other by the Summer School of the Royal Conservatory of Music. The main purpose of asking these three questions was to alert student teachers to the life-long effect of a child's early musical experiences, and to urge them to study developmentally appropriate methods and curriculum for the sensitive early years. 108 students between the ages of 20 and 35 were asked to write a short personal account of their *earliest, unhappiest* and *happiest* musical memories.

Subsequently, in a general discussion based on their reports, we noted that most of these remembered events happened from the early 1950's into the 1970's. We also noted that this period of time saw many changes in early childhood education, reflecting the research, the developmental studies and the philosophies of scholars such as Piaget, Montessori and Bruner. And during this same period, the concepts and pedagogy of music educators such as Jaques-Dalcroze, Orff and Kodaly were spreading around the music education world – through teacher's organizations such as I.S.M.E. But has contemporary thinking of Early Childhood Education influenced early childhood musical practices in the home and in the school? Perhaps the students' reports on the *earliest, unhappiest* and *happiest* musical memories will give us some clues. Listen to a few quotations from the students' earliest musical experiences, followed by some comment arising from their words:

- when 2-years-old "music at a family reunion . . . my uncles played on fiddles and guitars and my cousins and I danced with the music"

- when 3-years-old "listening to my Dad play the harmonica and my Mom sing"

- "singing song after song in bed with my three sisters"

- "my grandmother combing and braiding my hair, singing *Scarlet Ribbons*

There were many other responses such as these, which indicated the powerful impact of early informal musical play within the family group. Despite the growing encroachment during the 50's, 60's and 70's of commercial records, tapes, radio and television in the home, mass media experiences were seldom mentioned as an "earliest" experience. This confirmed our belief that informal music making within the family is the real beginning of music education. Teachers who direct stimulating music programmes with parents and young children are building a firm foundation on which to build future musical learning and understanding.

And now, let us hear some unhappy music experiences, from the earlier years:

- when 4-years-old "at a church picnic . . . I was given a drum to march in front of a band . . . I tried but could not march and play at the same time, so the drum was taken from me and I was excluded from the band"

- when 4-years-old "piano lessons . . . my teacher was strict, impersonal and frightening"

- when 5-years-old "I was in a musical skit and was left alone standing on the stage . . . I ran off in tears"

- "as a young child, I was asked by my Mother *not* to sing because I could not sing well"

- "I vividly remember my first piano teacher. She drank coffee and talked on the phone during my lesson. She also held my wrist and it hurt."

- "having to take piano lessons from a professor of music who was too advanced and had no patience"

These accounts included many other painful stories of children who were forced to play, sing or perform before they were developmentally ready. Some were physically or mentally abused by a music teacher and others were terrified by an examiner. We concluded that there were many teachers during this period who were unacquainted, unqualified or unimpressed by contemporary approaches to music education.

> "It is much more important who the singing master at Kisvärda (a village in Hungary) is than who the director of the opera house in Budapest is . . . for a poor director fails once, but a poor teacher keeps on failing for 30 years, killing the love of music in 30 classes of pupils." – *Zolton Kodaly*

Teachers of music must have an excellent music education, but they must have much more than musical knowledge. As well as a warm and understanding personality, the music teacher should have some professional knowledge of behavioural psychology, human growth and human development. The teacher should be able to understand and motivate the thinking and learning processes of young children. We must comprehend the joy of music in *the child's terms* and be able to nourish and encourage this special joy.

Here are some happy memories from children who have felt this special joy:

- "dancing in my backyard wearing only a nightgown . . . barefeet . . . hearing imaginary music"

- I loved singing with my kindergarten teacher"

- "singing around the campfire with my family"

- "the greatest enjoyment I can remember was when my piano teacher would play one of *my* pieces for me"

- "going back to my music teacher's house twenty years later for advice and reminiscence"

Other happy stories referred to satisfying solo or group performances with thrilling musical moments either as a performer or as a listener. Is this not the ultimate goal in our work as music educators – to turn young children toward music, to help them discover what music is through personal experience and then to encourage them to make their own music? This can be an exciting challenge for a teacher, but it is a difficult challenge, because young children do not perceive, feel or learn like older children. So we must gather, study and adapt methods and materials that will be effective in this work.

We look for the kind of musical learning that offers the greatest possibilities to the individual child. Outgoing physically active children may learn best with music and vigorous movement activities – they can have many musical experiences if the teacher is able to stimulate, direct and control this interest. Another child will find music in the sound and rhythms of speech. Some will discover the joy of singing and others will be stimulated when making sounds with instruments.

The student teachers concluded that an effective music curriculum should offer all of these activities so that all children can be turned toward music. The music teacher who has knowledge of Early Childhood Development can lead the child into many happy musical experiences which in time can foster a love of music that will stay with the child for a whole lifetime.

"The beginning is the most important part of the work."

Plato

Bibliography

Bruner, J.: **Toward A Theory of Instruction Harvard** University Press, 1971

Choksy, L., et al.: **Teaching Music in the 20th Century** Prentice Hall, 1986

Kodaly, Z.: **Selected Writings of Zolton Kodaly** Boosey & Hawkes, 1974

Montessori, M.: **Education for Human Development** Schocken Books, N.Y., 1976

Piaget, J.: **Psychology of Intelligence** Humanities Press, New Jersey, 1963

Sigel, I.: **The Piagetian System and the World of Education** from studies in Cognitive Development, Oxford University Press, 1969

Wood, D.: **Move, Sing, Listen, Play**, Gordon V. Thompson Music, Toronto, 1984 Revised edition 1995 by Gordon V. Thompson Music, A Division of Warner/Chappell Music Canada Ltd., Toronto, Canada

Zimmerman, M.: **The Relevance of Piagetian Theory for Music Education** International Journal for Music Education, No. 3, 1984